ANCHORED WITHIN THE VAIL

A Pictorial History of the Seamen's Church Institute

Leah Robinson Rousmaniere

*The author would like to thank
Carlyle Windley
without whose help, encouragement
and magnificent sense of humor
this book would not
have been possible.*

© 1995 The Seamen's Church Institute of New York and New Jersey
241 Water Street, New York, NY 10038, USA.

All rights reserved—no part of this book may be reproduced in any
form without written permission from the publisher, except by a
reviewer who wishes to quote brief passages in connection with
a review for inclusion in a magazine or newspaper.

Front cover photograph: New-York Historical Society
Back cover photograph: Courtesy of Esto Photographics,
© Jeff Goldberg/Esto
Book design by Sherry Streeter

ISBN 0-9643657-0-7

First printing
Printed in the United States of America

Contents

Chapter One	Finding Their Way	1
Chapter Two	Waterfront Reforms	22
Chapter Three	The Seamen's Church Institute Goes to War	38
Chapter Four	Mansfield's Dream Hotel	46
Chapter Five	The Second World War	70
Chapter Six	Sink or Swim	80
Chapter Seven	Sea Changes	98
	Bibliography	128
	Notes	131
	Photo credits	134

Foreword

It is difficult to discuss New York's maritime history without referencing the Seamen's Church Institute, for the two are inextricably linked. Indeed, the Institute in many ways helped to shape the growth of New York Port and will forever be a part of the history of this great port.

In 1834, New York was a bustling town and growing commercial center. It was home to some of America's most prosperous merchants, and the authors, journalists, and politicians of the day. That year, the people of the city also participated in their first mayoral election. At the heart of all this activity was the port, where tall-masted square riggers filled the harbor and ships of every size and rig lined the waterfront. It has been well documented that New York owes much of its success as a commercial city to the sheltered harbor and deep waters of the port.

Then, as now, seafarers were an integral part of the port's operation. On any given day more than 2,000 sea-hardened sailors roamed the city's streets. But the New York streets known by these merchant sailors were not paved in gold. The waterfront was littered with crimps and unscrupulous boardinghouse keepers who saw the sailors as easy prey and usually swindled them out of their hard-earned wages.

The Institute's founders believed that the seafarers' attentions could be diverted away from the dangers of the waterfront, if only there were other options. By 1843 they provided a port missioner to offer hospitality, assistance whenever possible, comfort and counsel to all seafarers regardless of rank, religion or nationality.

The Institute's mission since its founding rests on Biblical heritage that calls us all to protect the unprotected and to empower the weak. Hence, the Institute's early motto and title of this history book, *Anchored Within the Vail*, which was taken from a Methodist hymn.

Today, the Institute is the largest, most comprehensive seafarers' agency in North America. Operating in one of the world's most active ports, the Institute has seen the seafarer through many historic events. We recognize that world trade and the maritime tradition are a critical lifeline of peace and prosperity. We also understand that the seafarer stands at the center of this industry, and with the help of those who support us, the Institute will continue to serve merchant mariners of all nations.

The Reverend Peter Larom
Executive Director
Seamen's Church Institute of New York & New Jersey

CHAPTER ONE

Finding Their Way

The Reverend Benjamin C.C. Parker would later say that 1843 was a "highly interesting year."

That was the year things finally got off the ground at the "Young Men's Church Missionary Society," predecessor to the Seamen's Church Institute of New York and New Jersey.

For some time there had been rumblings of discontent among the members of the board of managers at "The Society." Too much talk, they grumbled. Not enough action. Not enough *focus*. "It is well known," the secretary of the Society's board later wrote, "that the '*Young Men's Church Missionary Society*' existed for a long time as an auxiliary to the City Mission Society, and that the results of that organization, though very important, were by no means equal to the wishes of its members. With all [the Society's] capabilities for effecting good, very much of its force was lost in fruitless discussion and enervated action, from the want of some definite object towards which to direct its undivided energies." It was all well and good to sponsor missionaries to far-flung Africa, and to the outposts of the wilds of New York state, and to the Tennessee frontier. But why not redirect the Young Men's energies to an *indigenous* group of destitute, a group languishing right under the Young Men's collective noses in the city and port of New York? Why not organize a mission to seafarers? The conviction grew that the Society was wasting time with talk and lack of focus. "This conviction," the secretary went on to explain, "together with the great spiritual destitution of Seamen in this city, determined that body upon reorganization and devotion of its whole strength to this much neglected portion of our fellow men."[1]

Board member Charles Tomes was the first to suggest that the Society address its energy and attention to the plight of seafarers. After sitting through four monthly meetings of the newly reconstituted and theoretically newly inspired Young Men's Church Missionary Society, and after reading aloud the decidedly uninspiring communiques from the secretary of the Domestic Board

The headquarters at 15 State Street

1

"View of the Harbor from Brooklyn Heights," unidentified artist, c. 1860

of Missions, the secretary of the Foreign Board of Missions, the missionary in Africa and the missionary in Tennessee, Tomes had had enough. Tomes put forward at the July 1842 monthly meeting the motion that the board appoint a committee of three to "inquire into the expediency of establishing a Mission to the Sailors in the City, and to report at the next meeting the best means of carrying the same into effect." The resolution was unanimously adopted. Charles Tomes, George T. Fox, Jr., and J. Rutsen Van Rensselaer were appointed to a three-man committee to look into the matter.[2] On November 24, 1842, a joint committee of the Young Men and the City Mission Society, their parent organization, succeeded in passing a resolution to establish an Episcopal Seamen's Mission in the Port of New York, thereby marking 1842 as the year the Protestant Episcopal Church of America undertook maritime mission work. And the documents committee — under George N. Titus's able direction — turned out an impressive amount of paperwork peppered with such words as *Resolved*, *Whereas*, *In-testimony-whereof*, and *Now-Know-Ye*.

But it wasn't until March 1843 (when members of the board tramped to their monthly meeting through thigh-high snowdrifts blown up the previous week by the worst storm in anyone's memory) that Van Rensselaer and two others managed to get the attention of the managers refocused on "the necessity of adopting some definite object for the future operation of the Society." The

Society's efforts, they urged, *must be concentrated on the establishment of a Sailors Mission*.[3] The ball began to roll, somehow. Committees were appointed anew, with fresh vigor: one committee to make inquiries regarding a space for a shore-side seamen's chapel to serve as an interim meeting place until the floating chapel the managers wanted could be built; and a second to interview candidates for the position of missionary to sailors.

Suddenly, the Society's secretary noted, "much of the right spirit was shown, which was a very cheering sign."[4]

It was a heady time in American history, a time of spiritual and social reform fueled — as one historian has written — by "the Puritan's compulsion to transform the world, the democratic American's conviction that men ought to be free, and the new Adam's soaring faith in human progress."[5] The evangelical resurgence of the Second Great Awakening was "refreshing" the country, another writer noted, and "God, in a remarkable manner, was pouring out his spirit on the churches."[6] Evangelism in its broadest, Utopian sense was intimately associated with moral reform and social benevolence. Before long, voluntary associations of missionary, reformatory, or benevolent purposes were springing up everywhere. "We are all a little wild here with numberless projects of social reform," Bostonian Ralph Waldo Emerson breathlessly wrote to his friend Carlyle in 1840, summing up the spirit of the age. "Not a reading man but has a draft of a new community in his waistcoat pocket."[7] Politically, it was the age of the common man; American political conservatives were swept aside by the tidal wave of the Log Cabin and Hard Cider campaign of 1840, and the colonial aristocracy of rank and station was disappearing in the wake of a meritocracy of entrepreneurship. Immigration, westward expansion, and an astonishing population explosion fired the can-do confidence of moving, moving forward. The new canals and railroads provided overland transportation, and steamships and fast clippers took cargo and passengers to domestic and foreign ports with a speed unimaginable only two decades earlier.

In 1843, the economic activity of the whole world passed in review along the wharves and in the countinghouses of New York City's South Street. Textiles from Manchester, tea from Canton, flour from Rochester, cotton from New Orleans all found their way to the great merchant houses on Pearl Street, and from there to buyers and sellers everywhere. There was scarcely a branch of American maritime activity in which the Port of New York did not participate and lead. Capitalizing on the ingenious innovation of regularly scheduled ocean-packet service in 1818, and the opening of the Erie Canal in 1825, New York had been able to draw trade from Europe at the expense of Boston and Philadelphia, her two nearest rivals in the shipping trades.

All of this bustling commerce depended on boats and ships. And the ships depended on the labor of the seafarers.

People of the times held divergent views of the seafarer's lot, as evidenced by the way they read Richard Henry Dana's *Two Years Before the Mast*, published in 1840. Some read it as romantic, high adventure — a young man's "triumphant,

The Reverend Benjamin C. C. Parker
First Missionary of the Society 1843-1859

Like many of the young men who made up the board of managers of the fledgling Society, Parker had found himself drawn to seafarers and their plight.

In 1841, the young priest was a passenger aboard a small packet sailing from Boston to New York City when the vessel, along with fifty others, was driven by contrary winds into a place called Tarpaulin Cove on the south shore of Naushon Island in Vineyard Sound.

Parker took the opportunity to organize a religious meeting on shore in the kitchen of a public house. Then he convinced a captain of a vessel anchored near Parker's own to send his boat among the vessels early the next morning to inform the officers and their crews that there would be a religious service on shore at 10 A.M.

"On the following morning there was almost a gale of wind," Parker wrote, "nevertheless these hardy fellows were true to their word. At eight o'clock I saw them on the top of mountain waves, floating like sea-gulls, going to the windward of the vessel, and passing word about our meeting." Once assembled for the service, "the poor sailors wept like children," inspiring Parker to continue his ministry with the crew aboard his ship. "We had reading of the Scriptures every night in the cabin, with explanations by me and prayers, which sometimes lasted an hour and a half."[8]

The experience made such an impression on Parker he was later able to pinpoint it as the occurrence that directed his mind to mission work with seamen. Arriving in New York shortly thereafter, he conferred with a few of the clergy and laymen in that great city and relayed his moving experiences.

Two years later, the board of managers of the Young Men's Church Missionary Society appointed him its first missionary to seafarers.

if temporary release from the constraints and artificiality of Brahmin Boston."[9] The reality of life at sea, however, was anything but romantic, and most readers of *Two Years Before the Mast* recognized it as an urgent call for amelioration of the condition of seamen. Emerson, commenting on his old pupil's book, was sure that it would "serve to hasten the day of reckoning between society and sailor."

The life of a merchant seafarer under sail was a hard one, with long hours and miserable conditions. The men risked their lives aloft in dangerous weather when one misstep could plunge them to the deck below or overboard to a watery grave in Davy Jones's locker. The captain was God and his order was law, and if the chief mate beat a few sailors black-and-blue while carrying it out, well, good discipline made for a smart ship. Life in the forecastle was bleak: damp and unheated, without amenities or rights. The sailors were expected to provide their own eating utensils, bed linen, and even the hard straw "donkey breakfast" that served as a mattress for the rough plank bunk. Food was routinely bad, a monotonous menu of "burgoo" (cornmeal mush served with molasses) for breakfast, and sea biscuit, or hardtack, with a little salt beef or salt pork, for dinner and supper. The biscuit was often full of weevils and so hard that one sailor in Melville's novel *Redburn* claimed to be able to tell the ages of seafarers by how far down their teeth had been worn by eating it.[10] Midshipmen in the British Royal Navy of the same time period put a new twist on the concept of "toying with your food" when they coaxed the maggots from their salt beef and saved them for maggot derbies.[11] This cheerless fare, moreover, was rationed, and a sailor who spilled his share while traversing the rolling deck from cookhouse to forecastle got no more until the next meal, although his watchmates usually contributed a spoonful each from their own portions so that the unlucky one would not go entirely without. When they were hungry, seafarers chewed tobacco to dull the pangs.

As remedy for this cruel exploitation, Richard Henry Dana, Jr. suggested legal aid to reform the sailors' condition aboard ship. But something also had to be done about the sailors' condition in port. For that, Dana suggested religious instruction to reform the sailors themselves.

Herman Melville was skeptical. Melville read *Two Years Before the Mast* before writing his novel *Redburn*, published in 1849, in which he also described a son-of-a-gentleman's first sea voyage. But he did not think wide-scale reformation of sailormen was possible. "The reflecting mind must very soon perceive that the case of sailors, as a class, is not a very promising one," he wrote. "The thought of lifting them up seems almost as hopeless as that of growing the grape in Nova Zembla."[12]

Clearly, the enthusiastic members of the board of managers of the Young Men's Church Missionary Society had their work cut out for them.

The merchants, businessmen, doctors, lawyers, and clergymen who made up the Society's membership had a lot to talk about, and discussions at the regular monthly meetings became very lively affairs, as can be seen by the minutes of the session on Monday, May 15, 1843.

First they needed to build a floating chapel.

No, first they needed to hire the missionary.

But the funds they had collected so far had been raised expressly for the purpose of procuring a vessel and building the chapel, as George T. Fox, Jr. pointed out patiently.

Henry Meigs argued that it was important to have the services of the missionary in *arranging for* the church, and that the missionary would be well employed preaching to sailors on the decks of the different vessels in the meantime.

Albert J. Journeay, Jr. reported on the hulk of a sloop he had looked at, the one that Robert Bowne Minturn was thinking of buying. Minturn — a name partner of Grinnell, Minturn & Company, whose blue and white swallowtail house flags flew over more than fifty vessels — had offered to present the sloop to the Society. But Journeay thought the sloop, at 145 tons, was too small.

The Reverend Dr. Gregory T. Bedell urged that they concentrate their

The Founding Board Members

The Reverend Smythe Pyne, president of the Young Men's Church Missionary Society through its reorganization as the Protestant Episcopal Church Missionary Society for Seamen. He is considered SCI's first president.

The members of the board of managers in 1843 were interesting and accomplished people. Their eclectic group included, among others:

The Reverend Dr. Gregory T. Bedell. Only twenty-six in 1843, he was one of the younger members of the board of managers. Then rector of the Church of the Ascension, Dr. Bedell later became bishop of Ohio.

The Reverend Dr. William D. Berrian. Called by the diarist George Templeton Strong "that amiable successor of the Apostles," Dr. Berrian was author of *The Sailors Manual of Devotion* and the rector at Trinity Church. In 1843, he was busy overseeing the construction of the new church, the previous edifice having been torn down in 1839 due to structural problems.

Andrew Haswell Green. In 1843 a twenty-three-year-old attorney, Green went on to become president of the New York Board of Education, commissioner of Central Park, and comptroller of the city, earning the appellation "Father of New York." He was also a founder of the Metropolitan Museum of Art in New York, the American Museum of Natural History, and the meteorological observatory.

William H. Hobart, J.D. Fitch, G.A. Sabine, C.D. Varley, and **Thomas Cook,** medical doctors.

Albert Journeay, Jr. Grandson of a French nobleman and Huguenot, son of an officer in the Revolutionary war, Journeay was head of his own firm, Albert Journeay, Jr. & Co. He was listed in *The Wealthy Citizens of New York*, which claimed he was worth at least $100,000.

The Reverend Lewis P.W. Balch, rector of St. Bartholomew's Church, and the **Reverend Samuel Lewis Southard, Jr.,** rector of Calvary Church.

Pierre E. F. McDonald. "Zealous for the church and devoted to the establishment of this mission, Pierre E.F. McDonald fell a martyr to its interests," the Society's secretary sadly noted. "Being one of a Committee specially intrusted with the planning and erection of the [Floating] Church, and in the discharge of his duty much exposed to the inclemency of the weather, he contracted a severe illness, which took him from us."[13]

George C. Morgan. A book merchant and stationer, Morgan served as vestryman at Trinity Church. He enjoyed sitting quietly or puttering about in the graveyard there, and after his death in 1862, his book, *Monuments and the Dead of Trinity Churchyard*, was published.

Henry Onderdonk. A distant cousin of the Right Reverend Henry U. Onderdonk, bishop of Pennsylvania, and his brother, the Right Rever-

George Titus

Captain Augustus Proal

end Benjamin T. Onderdonk, Bishop of New York, the Society's Henry Onderdonk was a schoolteacher whose great passion was the study of Long Island antiquities. He published a number of books on this topic.

Captain Augustus Proal. Master of the ship *Harkaway*, among others, Captain Proal affectionately encouraged his sailors to attend church while in port, and at sea officiated at religious services on the quarterdeck and weekly meetings for Bible reading and prayer in the cabin. The Reverend Dr. Charles J. Jones, a former seafarer who rose from debauchery to become chaplain of the Sailors' Snug Harbor on Staten Island, says Captain Proal gave him his first Bible.

James H. Ray. A former partner in the firm of Warner, Prall & Ray, pharmaceutical importers, in 1843 he was retired.

The Reverend Thomas H. Taylor, rector of Grace Church. Like Dr. Berrian at Trinity, in 1843 he was busy overseeing the construction of a new church building.

J. Rutsen Van Rensselaer, Sr. A former member of the New York State legislature who had been associated with Governor DeWitt Clinton in the building of the Erie Canal, Van Rensselaer in 1843 was seventy-six years old. He had shared in all the Society's changes since its foundation as the Young Men's Auxiliary Education and Missionary Society, was a prominent mover in its several reorganizations, and actively took part in planning, building, and launching the Floating Chapel. He died in 1846, and "the loss of his mild and discreet counsels" was greatly mourned by the Society.[14] Van Rensselaer's son Jeremiah, who was interested in railways and founder of Dodd's Express, also served on the board.

The Reverend Dr. Henry J. Whitehouse. Rector of St. Thomas's Church and afterwards the second Protestant Episcopal bishop of Illinois, Dr. Whitehouse was admired as one of the most elegant prelates of his time. As bishop, he was responsible for the adoption of the cathedral system in this country, and he founded the cathedral of St. Peter and St. Paul in Chicago. A personal friend of the archbishop of Canterbury, Whitehouse once preached before Queen Victoria in the Chapel Royale. His son, Francis M. Whitehouse, later served on the board of the Institute, and he and his wife built the thirteenth floor of 25 South Street during the First World War as a memorial to their son Meredyth.

George Norton Titus. A lawyer of the firm of Cleveland and Titus in New York, Titus was one of the incorporators of the nascent Society and an originator of the idea of a floating church for seafarers. He served as a lay vice president from 1843 to 1845. He had three daughters, Mrs. William Harman Brown, Mrs. Tompkins Westervelt, and Mrs. John A. Aspinwall. The chancel rail in the second chapel at 25 South Street was given by their children, Helen Stewart and Edith Harman Brown, in memory of their grandfather.

Thomas P. Cummings. Twenty-eight years of age in 1843, an original incorporator and the first recording secretary of the Society, Cummings was reelected a lay manager from year to year until his death in 1894. In 1861, he became a vice president, and he was treasurer from 1870 to 1873. His son, Charles F. Cummings, served on the board from 1892 to 1909 and was followed by *his* son, Frederick A. Cummings.

The Reverend Smythe Pyne, president of the Young Men's Church Missionary Society through its reorganization as the Protestant Episcopal Church Missionary Society for Seamen. He is considered SCI's "first" president.

These men were the clerical vice presidents, lay vice presidents, and managers of the Young Men's Church Missionary Society. They attended meetings, appointed one another to committees, and did the everyday volunteer work of the Society.

In 1894, when the fiftieth anniversary of the Society was celebrated, original incorporators Thomas P. Cummings, John Davenport, Edward M. Duncan, and Frederick H. Trowbridge were still around to join in the festivities.

SOUTH STREET, 1828

Along this street SCI's board of managers conducted their business: Grinnell, Minturn & Company, merchants (part of the land on which the Institute would stand from 1913 to 1968 was held under a benefaction of Robert Bowne Minturn); Schermerhorn, Banker & Company, ship chandlers (Schermerhorn's great-great-grandson, Colonel Arthur Schermerhorn, would serve on the Institute's board of managers in the 1930s and 1940s); and Wetmore & Cryder (Wetmore's family would later give the officers' dining room to the building at 25 South Street).

efforts on the hiring of the missionary.

Too small? Pierre E.F. McDonald interjected, ignoring the good Reverend Doctor. A sloop that size could be fitted up to seat 400 persons!

Henry Fisher agreed. That sloop couldn't possibly be as contemptible an affair as some people are making her out to be, he said. Better to commence at once! Some of our largest congregations commenced in a very small way.

And so on. The only thing the members of the board could agree on that evening was "to adjourn to this day fortnight."

Yet six weeks later, on July 3, 1843, the newly hired seamen's chaplain was in place. He was the Reverend Benjamin Clarke Cutler Parker, a Protestant Episcopal priest, Harvard '22, son of the Right Reverend Samuel Parker, D.D.,

FINDING THEIR WAY

Unsafe pleasures. Seafarers carouse at John Allen's, a popular Sailortown dance hall.

Map of lower Manhattan in the 1840s, showing Sailortown

SEAMEN'S CHURCH INSTITUTE

CAPTAIN CHARLES HENRY MARSHALL

During the 1820s and 1830s a ship captain, Marshall founded and operated the Black Ball Steamship Line, whose packet ships traveled the first scheduled route from New York to Liverpool, England. When he retired, he came ashore and dedicated himself to ameliorating the condition of seafarers.[15] His grandson and namesake, Charles H. "Buddy" Marshall, served on the Institute's board from 1943 until his death in 1952, and his stepson, the Honorable Anthony D. Marshall, became president of SCI in 1980.

Captain Charles Henry Marshall (from a portrait owned by his grandson, Charles H. Marshall). Today, Mrs. Janos Scholz and Mrs. Anna Glen Vietor, both descendants of Marshall, continue to be active in support of SCI's work.

second Bishop of Massachusetts. In his mid-forties, the sandy-haired clergyman had previously officiated at Christ Church in Gardiner, Maine; Trinity Church in Lenox, Mass.; St. James Church in Woodstock, Vermont; and St. George's Church in Flushing, Long Island, New York. He was about to officiate in "an unattractive room over a grog shop"[16] at the corner of Pike and South Streets, which he had just rented as a temporary chapel.

Undoubtedly this was the moment when Reverend Parker decided 1843 was turning out to be a highly interesting year.

The first service in the new Seamen's Episcopal Chapel over the grog shop was held on July 17, 1843, with Parker officiating. "About one hundred persons present. Preserved Fish, his wife, and numerous other respectable people present. About 15 or 20 sailors were also on hand," Parker wrote in his journal.[17]

Despite the many honored guests, one can only imagine the decorum or lack thereof at this first service. The new Seamen's Episcopal Chapel on the corner of Pike and South was located in the heart of Sailortown, "where the lanes were the darkest and filthiest, where the dens were the deepest and foulest, where the low bar-rooms, groggeries, and dance-houses were the most numerous, where the vilest women and men abided, in the black sea of drunkenness, lewdness, and sin," and where — at least according to one account — brawls, rioting, robberies, and murders took place daily.[18] The chapel's South Street neighbors included (besides the grog shop) a blacksmith, shipjoiners, and blockmakers, whose din mingled with that of the piano players of the dance houses, the one difference being that the blacksmith, shipjoiners, and blockmakers probably went to sleep at night, whereas the piano players didn't. All night long, the sound of revelry, shouts of the drunken, and "oaths of reeking blasphemy" could be heard.

RAINBOW

When the *Rainbow*, generally regarded by modern authorities as the first of the extreme clippers, left New York on her maiden voyage to Canton, China, on February 1, 1845, the Reverend Benjamin C.C. Parker was one of those invited by William H. Aspinwall (an early patron of the Society) to join the owner's and builder's party and ride with the ship out to Sandy Hook. After all sails had been set and the ship was standing out to sea, the captain called the men who could be spared from the sheets —close to fifty of them—back around the after hatch. He then requested Parker to make a short prayer, "commending us all on this voyage to the protection of Almighty God." After the benediction, the great clipper slowed to steerageway off the Hook with her main sails aback, the visitors debarked into a steamboat that had been hired for the occasion, and, as Parker recorded in his journal for that day, "the beautiful ship, with six cheers from her crew, bore away, presenting one of the finest sights that ever delighted the eyes of a sailor, or did honor to architects or owners."[19]

At least 2,000 seafarers were in port at any one time, most of them thronging Sailortown. Parker estimated only one-fifth of them to be Americans — the rest "English, Dutch, Swedish, Germans, Danes, Scandinavians, and some few Spanish, French, and Portuguese, which are generally Catholics." He also gloomily noted, "Few of the latter can read. None want Bibles or tracts."[20]

Indeed, attempts to minister to the seafaring community so far had not achieved the desired results. Early on, those who wished to help the poor had recognized seafarers as worthy of charity, and societies promoting the welfare of sailors had sprung up in all the world's major ports, including the American ports of Boston, Philadelphia, Baltimore, Charleston, New Orleans, and New York, among others.[21] By 1825, there were seventy Bethel unions, thirty-three marine bible societies, and fifteen seamen's churches and floating bethels (chapels) throughout the world — including the shore-based operations in the American ports of Boston, Philadelphia, Baltimore, Charleston, New Orleans, and others.

CRIMPS

From necessity or choice, ship captains played into the hands of these desperadoes, soliciting them for sailors to fill out short-handed crews and then turning a blind eye when said sailors arrived aboard ship. Melville describes the typical scene: "Several of the sailors were very drunk, and one was lifted on board insensible by his landlord, who carried him down below and dumped him into a bunk."[22] When the seafarer awoke from his debauch, finding himself without clothing, friendless and penniless, he frequently did not even know who shipped him, what ship he was on, or where he was going.

Crimps hoist an unconscious seafarer aboard.

The New York Port Society, founded in 1818 by a small group of merchants and shipbuilders "for promoting the gospel among seamen," had opened the nondenominational Mariner's Church in 1820 but had then floundered on and off due to "pecuniary embarrassment." The American Seamen's Friend Society was established in 1826 "to improve the social and moral condition of seamen by uniting the efforts of the wise and good in their behalf," but it made little headway with seafarers. A problem shared by all seamen's societies was the religious tracts some published. Heavily larded with legalism and moralism, they could not establish any real rapport with seafarers. "About this new fangled society. . . . what the devil are they going to do with us? Make us all saints and deacons?" one old tar wanted to know, complaining about the Boston Society for the Religious and Moral Improvement of Seamen.[23]

Also antagonistic to the societies' efforts were the "land sharks" and "crimps." From the earliest times in England, merchant seamen, fishermen, and landlubbers had been press-ganged for service in the Royal Navy; by the turn of the 19th century, the kidnapping of seamen to serve as crews in the merchant fleets of the world had become a recognized evil. In sailortowns worldwide, the "Shanghai fraternity" of crimps — boardinghouse keepers, rogue tailors, shipping-masters, runners, draymen, and boatmen — flourished to rob Sailor Jack of his hard-earned cash.

Because ships took from seven to ten days after arriving in port to "pay off" seamen, a sailor first came ashore without a penny in his pocket. After a long, "dry" voyage, during which he had endured dangerous conditions, hunger, cold, a most difficult and spartan life, and more often than not a crazed bucko mate

THE *KEYING*

Parker combined religious and practical assistance to distressed seamen. One example of this was the flamboyant rescue of the shanghaied Chinese seamen on the British-owned junk *Keying*.

In 1847, when Captain Kellett's *Keying* arrived in New York from Canton, the crew sent word to a Chinese mandarin visiting New York that they had been shanghaied. The mandarin appealed to several merchants for help, who in turn appealed to Parker and retired Captain Richardson, president of the American Seamen's Friend Society. A lawsuit was brought against Captain Kellett and the junk was seized. The Chinese seamen were brought ashore and housed in the Sailors' Home operated by Captain Richardson, and Kellett agreed to pay the seamen's back wages and passage back to Canton. Parker invited the sailors to visit the Floating Church and arranged for them to be provided with copies of *The Life of John Newton*, engravings of the interior and exterior of the Floating Church, and red flannel shirts for the rounding of Cape Horn.

The bay and harbor of New York, 1847, with the *Keying* in the background

While the Chinese seamen—who did not speak English—might have wondered what to do with their copies of *The Life of John Newton* and engravings of the Floating Church, they were immeasurably helped by the legal aid and warm clothing. And Parker's pragmatism in addressing seamen's social needs set the tone for the fledgling Society.[24]

hell-bent on attacking the men with belaying pins, Sailor Jack was ready to enjoy his newfound freedom and luxuriate in a little wine, woman, and song. But he had no money until payday.

Here the crimps came in. As soon as a ship was reported off a port, boatmen would row the runners out. Boarding the vessel by means of grapnels — often before she even dropped anchor — the runners would "go into the fo'c'sle, give the cock of the fo'c'sle a golden guinea, or a dollar, get all hands half-soused, and, probably, go aloft with the crowd to help them store the 'muslin.'"[25] Offering the gullible sailor — besides booze — celestial delights, gambling, and girls, the runners blithely waved aside payment until after payday. All could be had on credit. Money? Not a problem. The crimps would advance Jack a little pocket money until he was paid and run up a bill against him on credit for food, lodgings, and clothing. "The money accruing, therefore, from a winter voyage around the Horn or across the Atlantic fell by power of attorney, or a less legal instrument, to the boarding-house keeper," one writer noted. "If the bill represented a larger amount than the wages, Jack was shipped off at once, an advance note, payable several days after the sailing, having also been extorted from him."[26]

Frequently Jack was shipped off drugged; the doping of seamen was practiced from earliest times along the New York waterfront and throughout Sailortown. At first it was tobacco dottle and opium dregs, later real opium, morphine laudanum, or hydrate of chloral. More frequently, Jack was shipped off dead drunk.

Occasionally he was shipped off dead. The crimp would drench in rum some dead body, stolen from a morgue or killed in a street fight, and then ship it out as a drunken sailor — obtaining, as usual, the 'man's' advance note (very often equaling two months' wages), which he would cash before the ship's afterguard found out that the supposedly drunken sailor was actually a dead one.[27]

Parker's journal is full of accounts of sailors abused by the crimps, including a lengthy account of seaman Walter George Haynes, from Mississippi, who came to Parker "in his summer clothes, the only garments he owned, and in these he must go to sea while the mercury was at zero, in the dead of winter." Moreover, Parker added sadly, "He was in debt for two weeks board and his advance wages would all go to his landlord, when he found a ship for him. In this state he must suffer intensely. It is only one of many such cases, which we daily see and cannot relieve."[28]

While the Society would later come to address both the legal and social welfare of its seafaring constituents, in the fall of 1843 the board members concentrated on building a floating chapel to address their spiritual needs. A delegation was sent to Brooklyn to re-inspect the hull of the ferryboat *Manhattan* — a "double boat" (catamaran) thirty feet in width, seventy feet in length, "Copper and Copper fastened, apparently perfectly tight, and for all purposes of a Floating Chapel as good as any bottom." Board members Augustus Proal and Henry Fisher bought her for four hundred dollars — actually three hundred and fifty dollars after the sellers chipped in fifty dollars as a donation to the cause.[29]

At a meeting on Thursday evening, October 26, 1843, Charles H. Simonson of the shipjoiner's yard Bishop & Simonson — builders of the *Lexington* in 1835 and subsequently well known for the many steam vessels built there — personally presented his plans for the floating chapel to the committee. The members, impressed and excited, signed a contract to build the nation's first floating sanctuary.

Four months later, the Floating Church of Our Saviour for Seamen was commissioned and towed to Whitehall Slip at the tip of Manhattan. A pinnacled, Gothic-style church, with a seventy-foot steeple, it was a stunning and entirely novel form of ecclesiastical maritime architecture, plunked down onto a simple

The (First) Floating
Church of Our Saviour

deck stretched across the two catamaran-type hulls of the former ferryboat. The exterior was covered in cedar boards, painted a dark stone color, and sanded over, while the inside had been ingeniously decorated with a *trompe l'oeil* groined ceiling complete with Gothic moldings and recesses. St.-Mark's-in-the-Bowery donated a beautiful marble baptismal font in the form of a capstan, capped by a scallop shell to hold the holy water. (This baptismal font now stands in a prominent position in the chapel at the Institute's Water Street headquarters.) And there was a "fine-toned organ to lead them in the performance of their chants, and in singing in the Church service." Some 12,000 admiring sailors and landspeople came on board during three days of public viewing, after which the chapel was towed — with great fanfare — to its home berth in the East River at the foot of Pike Street. Among the guests invited to sail 'round in it were about fifty women, many belonging to New York's first families, and one hundred and seventy seamen. At the service concluding the festivities, as described in a contemporary publication, all rose and gave a resounding rendition of "Old Hundred," and "the voices of the ladies were sweetly mingling with those of the weather-beaten tars. . . ."[30]

The new chapel was an immediate success. Soon *The Evergreen* was able to report that on Sunday mornings, "from two to three hundred seamen, with as many more persons of their family or friends, or individuals interested in them, are regularly assembled, making a congregation of from four to six hundred; a more promiscuous congregation of ladies and gentlemen, being mingled with the sons of the ocean in the afternoon."[31] During services sailors were encouraged to send forward notes to be read aloud, and many availed themselves of this opportunity. They asked the prayers of the congregation that God preserve them from the dangers of the deep, or they thanked God for a safe return to port, or offered praise for recovery from illness.

The Floating Chapel was not without its problems. Despite published assurances that worshippers should experience no inconvenience beyond "a little undulation," Parker confided in his diary that during high winds the rolling motion of the chapel could become so pronounced that "many were seasick and went out." He himself sometimes found it difficult to keep his balance during communion. Occasionally, the chapel was rammed by ships maneuvering in the river. Once, weighted down by a heavy snowfall, the chapel sank to the riverbed. Parker galvanized a group of workers to raise it again, and the following Sunday he preached on the text of — appropriately — "Hold thou me up and I shall be safe."

Proud of their new Floating Chapel and inspired by a heady sense of accomplishment, the managers of the Young Men's Church Missionary Society decided to reorganize. The time had come for them to operate independently of their parent organization, the City Mission Society.

On April 12, 1844, the Young Men obtained a charter as the "Protestant Episcopal Church Missionary Society for Seamen in the City and Port of New York."

The Society had begun its corporate existence.

SCI'S SECOND FLOATING CHAPEL, 1846

During its first half century, the Protestant Episcopal Society for Seamen expanded and diversified its activities. In 1846, the board rejoiced in the launching of a second floating chapel, the Floating Church of the Holy Comforter, to serve the Hudson River — then still called the North River — at the foot of Dey Street. A second missionary was hired; the Reverend Daniel Van Mater Johnson joined Chaplain Parker in his work along the waterfront. For many years the two floating chapels continued as the mainstay of the Society's mission to seafarers, until 1866, when, after twenty-three years of service as a spiritual refuge for untold thousands of sailors, the Floating Church of

Floating Church of the Holy Comforter

The Vanderbilt windows. In 1888, funds from the legacy of William H. Vanderbilt, son of Cornelius, provided for the windows of the Society's brick Church of the Holy Comforter. The windows were later moved to the Institute's Chapel of Our Saviour at 25 South Street, and from there to the Institute's chapel at 15 State Street.

Second Floating Church of our Saviour, moored at the foot of Pike Street

Our Saviour was declared unseaworthy and had to be abandoned. Services were temporarily transferred to rooms at 62 Pike Street until another floating church, also called the Floating Church of Our Saviour, could take its place. In 1868, with deep regret, the board voted to abandon the Floating Church of the Holy Comforter, which had also reached an advanced state of decay. This chapel was not replaced. The Society leased rooms at 75 Beach Street, where the new idea of an "institutional" church began to germinate.

Having recognized the need to help seamen in "both body and soul," the board as early as 1850 approved a modest beginning for a sailors' home at 2 Carlyle Street, to be operated by the Reverend Daniel V.M. Johnson

The North River Station: Church of the Holy Comforter for Sailors

Right—The Breakwater in Brooklyn

Below—The reading room in the Breakwater

Below left—The reading room at 34 Pike Street

Below right—East Side Missionary House at 34 Pike Street

"Laid up for winter — Canal Boat Colony in Coenties Slip, East River"

and several lay members of the Society. Later that year, the home moved to larger quarters at 107 Greenwich Street. Called variously the Seamen's Home or Mariner's Home, this lodging house during 1851 accommodated more than 500 men. In addition, it fed sixty penniless sailors without charge, clothed fifty-five men, and — Johnson proudly reported — weaned seventy-five from booze. It also provided a lending library and a rudimentary banking service: Arrangements were made to accept deposits for the Seamen's Bank for Savings, and sailors staying at the home during 1852 deposited $7,589.79 for safekeeping or forwarding to relatives. Soon even larger quarters were required; in October 1854, the Society opened the New Sailors' Home at 338 Pearl Street on Franklin Square, and was soon lodging a thousand sailors a year. A four-story building with accommodations for seventy-five men, it was operated as a concession by proprietor John Marett. Thus began in these modest settings the institutional church work of lodging seafarers that would later evolve into the Seamen's Church Institute at 25 South Street.

With great prescience, the board envisioned, in its Annual Report of 1854, an as-yet-hypothetical home for sailors where "the Library and reading room, the Nautical Free School and Lecture Room, the Office of Intelligence, where [the sailor] may obtain reliable information; the intercourse and society of the intelligent, the honest and kind, may influence and elevate his intellectual and moral being." Step by step, the board set out to accomplish this. By the 1880s, the hypothetical was well on its way to being realized: For $29,000, the board purchased a property with frontage on both Houston and West Streets, and eight years later, they could proudly survey not only their Sailors' Home, but a brand new "institute" to complement it: the North River Station, including a brick building with a belfry, the new Church of the Holy Comforter (consecrated on March 18, 1888), and a rectory.

The reading room of the North River Station provided a vista of the Cunard docks, and it was men and officers of the "North Atlantic Ferry" — the great French and English steam liners — who took most advantage of the new institute. As many of the liners had "fou-fou" hands — crewmen who produced music of sorts from harmonicas, Jews' harps, washboards, kettles, and other makeshift instruments — there was plenty of talent for evening entertainment at the station. On one occasion, a troupe of ten seamen from the British liner *Cedric*, billed as "the *Cedric* Follies," entertained with songs, skits, and clog dancing, much to the delight of a packed house. More than 100 seamen used the reading rooms every day. Stranded and jobless seamen found refuge there, and the employment bureau found jobs for them.

Meanwhile, in 1868 the Society had also purchased an old house at 34 Pike Street for $13,000, completely remodeling it to serve as a mission, with reading room, lecture room, and a residence for the East River missionary. It had opened in 1869. The reading room was well stocked with English and foreign-language newspapers and periodicals, also a library of several hundred books. A mailing service was initiated whereby seafarers could use 34 Pike Street as their mailing address and have mail held for them for a considerable period; thus, a small start was made in a very important branch of missionary activity, which would blossom in 1913 into the full-fledged post office at the new Institute at 25 South Street. In 1899, the Seamen's Branch of the Legal Aid Society, sponsored by the Joint Conference of Seamen's Societies, would begin its career at 34 Pike Street. Between March 1899 and December 1, 1900, the attorney, Clark H. Abbott, would receive 5,778 applications from seamen for legal aid.

In addition to the North River Station and the East River Station, the Society since 1852 had operated a third station in the area of Whitehall at Coenties (pronounced co-EN-teez) Slip. Coenties Slip, as the Society's Annual Report of 1878 noted, contained "the largest floating population of any other street or slip along the East River. This large moving mass are nearly all dependent on the water for a living — seamen, boatmen, bargemen, truckmen who receive and deliver goods alongside the shipping, longshoremen who load and unload the vessels."[32] Much of the work here was directed toward the "canallers," the men who skippered the fleet of canal boats that were towed by steamboat between New York and Albany. They lived on board, year-round, with their wives and children.

The Coenties Slip Station was an outdoor enterprise from the start, with the Society's third missionary, the Reverend E.F. Remington, preaching in the open in the tradition of Christianity's "apostolic age." Even after the Society leased a room at 21 Coenties Slip to serve as a reading room, services continued to be held outside on nearby Pier Six, under a donated marquee tent large enough to shelter three hundred persons, equipped with benches to seat most of that number. In 1858, the Reverend Robert Walker became chaplain of the Coenties Slip post and introduced another service for seamen — regular visits to the hospitals. "There were," he reported to the board of managers, "a great many sailors laid up in hospitals and most of them quite friendless and helpless." Bit by bit the Society was expanding from the old concept of the seamen's Bethel to a broader scope of service, more "institutional" in nature.

In 1872, Coenties Slip Station was taken over by the Reverend Isaac Maguire, a six-foot Irishman with a booming brogue and kindly sense of humor. Maguire, in diary-scribbling, Parkerian tradition, chronicled some of the station's more colorful aspects. About his congregants, he said, they "adapt their costume to the temperature of the weather," and were "supremely indifferent to the opinions which those of more refinement and taste may form of their appearance."[33] Some were disruptive. From time to time, wrote Maguire, "a son of Neptune, top heavy from too much drink, comes rolling along and wishes to be heard and seen. He is generally easily subdued and if not induced to go his way sits down on the string piece of the pier, or on one of the benches under the tent, and takes the gospel as he takes his liquor, without regard to form or ceremony."

Then there were the whims and vagaries of weather: In his diary entry for August 19, 1883, Maguire tells how, just at the close of prayer, a sudden gust of wind swept the mission tent from above their heads onto the canal boats tied up nearby; then, "the thunder roared and the rain fell, which completely scattered the congregation."[34] Apparently events of this kind were not uncommon. "An invigorating place of worship," the *New York Times* commented in 1897.[35]

CHAPTER TWO

Waterfront Reforms

A self-proclaimed "cuss," the Reverend Archibald Romaine Mansfield set his jaw. The course of action, as he proposed it, was clear: "to do for the sailor's good exactly what the crimps had been doing for his harm. They were the first to greet him in the harbour; so should we. They offered him friendship and advice; so should we. They stood by him at the pay-off and took his money; so should we [for safekeeping]. They arranged for his food, lodging, clothing and amusements; so should we. They provided him a gathering-place for companionship and social life; so should we. Finally, they got work for him when he signed off; *so should we.*"[36]

Hired in 1896 by the Society to run the East River Station, Mansfield, a year after his arrival, horrified the board of managers by becoming embroiled in what the *New York Times* called "the Shipowners' War" and Mansfield called "the war against the crimps." As he later described it, "They hauled me over the coals for risking the good name of our society over what could so easily be made to appear as nothing better than a disgraceful street-row."[37] But Mansfield was someone for whom a good street-row had a certain appeal. Indeed, he'd taken the job at the Society in the first place because "I could see that it meant a lively fight, and that just suited me, because I liked to fight."[38] What they needed most, Mansfield felt, was to change the laws.

Federal legislation on behalf of seafarers prior to 1898 had been unsuccessful. The Shipping Commissioner's Act of 1872, signed into law on June 7, 1872, provided for the appointment of shipping commissioners in the various ports to regulate the hiring and "paying off" of seamen. "Before its passage ship's articles could be signed anywhere, on board ship, in the owner's offices, in 'tailor-shops,' or on the wharves," Mansfield later explained. "When men could not be got any other way, it was perfectly practicable to carry them on board forcibly, or in an unconscious state, i.e., to shanghai them. The Shipping Commissioner's Act

South Street at Cuyler's Alley, 1890

The Young Mansfield

On the morning of his twenty-fifth birthday, January 3, 1896, seminarian Archibald R. Mansfield assumed formal charge of the Society's East River Station. Hired purely on faith by Benoni Lockwood, a lay vice president of the Society, and by Edmund L. Baylies, a member of the board of managers who'd had only two questions for the gangly, would-be cleric ("Can you swim? Can you sail a boat?" — the answer was *no* on both counts), Mansfield was appointed superintendent within two years. Energetic and tenacious, he immediately reorganized the Society and became involved with waterfront reforms.

Archibald Mansfield in his seminary days

---

sought to abolish shanghaiing by ruling that seamen on American ships must sign their articles before a United States Shipping Commissioner, and that only sober men could sign; and furthermore that seamen were to be paid their wages in person."[39] There were many provisions in the act describing in great detail the signing and discharging of seamen; defining their rights and duties; their relationship to the ships and to its owner and officers; and prescribing penalties for desertion.

The crimps and shipping masters in New York, incensed by the Shipping Commissioner's Act, quickly leagued together into an organization they called "The Benevolent Society of Boarding House Keepers in the Port of New York" and refused to furnish crews. Shipping stopped dead; not a sailor was to be found. As Mansfield later pointed out, the crimps "were able to make so much trouble in the matter of getting crews that owners and officers were pretty well ready to connive at their lawbreaking, and nobody else was enough interested to oppose them."[40] In June 1874, the crimps were further abetted by an amendment of the act so that it applied only to deep-sea crews, but not the coastwise or lake-going trade. The law of 1872 was simply too complicated for short runs.

Besides, by that time the crimps had the situation sussed. Only a sailor who is sober can sign? They sent a laudably sober sailor around to sign articles before the commissioners, "then put on board whatever human material they had on hand and wanted to get rid of when sailing day came," Mansfield snorted.[41] Some sober-looking seamen were prevented from shipping out when they wanted, instead recruited by the crimps on a semi-permanent basis for this scam. In 1883, one able-bodied seaman signed the roll from a boardinghouse on Water Street twelve times before being permitted to sail on the *Thomas H. Lord III* of Baltimore for San Francisco.[42]

Another comprehensive act on behalf of seamen's rights, the Maguire Act of 1895, abolished imprisonment for desertion in the coastwise trade. This act passed into law the same year four sailors shipped in the *Arago* out of San Francisco and thence to Chile. Mansfield tells us, "Dissatisfied with conditions

J. AUGUSTUS JOHNSON

Born in 1836 in Boston, the son of a Methodist clergyman, John Augustus Johnson was apprenticed to a merchant prince but ran away to sea. Thus began an illustrious career among sailors, which, after a roundabout digression into the foreign service, would culminate in a vocation of tireless and triumphant advocacy on behalf of seafarers' rights.

In 1882, Johnson was elected as lay manager to the board of managers of the "Society for Seamen," as the Institute was then informally called. It was as chairman of the Society's committee on legislation that he undertook his aggressive campaign to ameliorate the condition of seamen, pushing through Congress the comprehensive White Bill, which passed into law as "An act to amend the laws relating to American seamen, for the protection of such seamen, and to promote commerce," on December 21, 1898.

About this act — probably the singularly most important piece of legislation on behalf of seafarers — Mansfield would later write, "I think it is no exaggeration to say that [Johnson] was the one man responsible for the passage of the bill in its final form."[43] Johnson was also instrumental in setting up a Seamen's Branch of the Legal Aid Society, which distinguished New York for its legal protection of seafarers; even as late as 1914, seamen said that nowhere else on the fringes of the seven seas were their rights so fully guarded as in New York.

---

on board the *Arago*, and believing that the Maguire Act gave them full choice in the matter, the sailors left the ship in Washington and went down to Oregon, where they were jailed until the *Arago* was ready to sail, and they were forcibly put on board by the United States Marshal. They refused to work, were put in irons until the ship returned to San Francisco, where they were taken off and lodged in jail."[44] In January 1897, the Supreme Court ruled that although the seafarers had deserted in a United States port, they had shipped for a foreign port and were therefore not protected under the Maguire Act. Moreover, while the Thirteenth Amendment prohibited involuntary servitude, the provisions did not apply to these men, since their case was exceptional. "The contract of the sailor has been treated as an exceptional one, involving to a certain extent the surrender of his personal liberty during the life of the contract," Justice Harlan, writing for the Court, claimed. Besides, American seamen were determined "deficient in that full and intelligent responsibility for their acts which is accredited to ordinary adults and as needing the protection of the law in the same sense which minors and wards do."[45] A howl of injustice went up from the seamen's unions at this "second Dred Scott decision," as it was rightly called.

But the decision did have one salutary effect: It "precipitated all the humanitarian sentiment in the country on behalf of fair dealing with the sailor," Mansfield wrote.[46] Propitiously, this sentiment occurred precisely at the right moment. The building of trade unions among seafarers had begun after the Civil War, and in 1878 the Lakes Seamen's Union, the first seafarer's labor organization of consequence in this country, was founded. Several others followed, and by 1897 the Coast Seamen's Union, under the powerful and fair leadership of Andrew Furuseth, had managed to get two bills into committee in Congress. Because of the *Arago* debacle, public opinion became focused on them.

"The time had come for general unified action by all the organizations directly or indirectly interested in the sailor's welfare, in attacking the one primary problem of maritime law," Mansfield decided. "Until this was done, nothing could be done that in the long run would be worth doing." He later elaborated:

> Our problem had several sides. First, the sailor needed a special form of legal protection, on account of the nature of his work. Laws which were adequate for the protection of a land-status were not sufficient to protect a sea-status. Second, the existing laws which recognized his special status were in many respects antiquated and needed revising. Third, the laws which applied to his welfare were pretty regularly disregarded and needed enforcing. Fourth, and most important, the national conscience and the civic conscience of the Port of New York needed awakening to these facts.[47]

With these goals in mind, the twenty-seven-year-old Mansfield acquired a powerful ally.

J. Augustus Johnson, lay manager and chairman of the Society's committee on legislation, was an impassioned champion of seamen's legislation and had been for some years. Formerly consul general at Beirut (then in Ottoman-controlled Syria), Johnson had served — under the Treaty of Extraterritoriality with Turkey — as judge in all cases involving American citizens. During this stint of adjudication, Johnson dealt with numerous complaints by seamen against their masters, and it became clear to him that, while the dictatorial powers enjoyed by a ship's captain were necessary for discipline and safety at sea, inadequate safeguards had been provided to protect men before the mast against the abuse of these powers. He determined that as soon as circumstances permitted, he would devote himself to the improvement of maritime law bearing upon the condition of the sailor. Admirably suited for the work through his government connections, Johnson became an effective advocate of reform legislation before administrative departments and legislative committees in Washington.[48]

Johnson agreed with Mansfield: Unified action had to be mustered. He set about approaching the various societies for seamen in New York. Together with Dr. W.C. Stitt, secretary of the American Seamen's Friend Society, Johnson organized a meeting of delegates from the American Seamen's Friend Society, the Christian Endeavor Seamen's Bethel Union, the Maritime Association, and the Marine Society. At the initial meeting, on January 9, 1897, the Joint Conference of Seamen's Societies was formed to discuss matters that might be of interest to the member societies.

Whatever initial momentum the conference achieved, however, quickly disintegrated into waffling and procrastination. Johnson's high hopes that the

ANDREW FURUSETH

Hailed often as the "Lincoln of the Sea" and described by one writer as "a former shellback with the face, voice, and force of an Old Testament prophet,"[49] "St. Andrew" at the turn of the century was president of the International Seamen's Union and devoted most of his life to obtaining better conditions for American seamen. When threatened with imprisonment for violation of an injunction during a strike in 1904 in San Francisco, Furuseth defiantly announced in his thick Norwegian accent, "I put my inyunction in my pocket and to go yail." His further proclamation, oft-quoted as a rallying cry for seafarers everywhere, has been subsequently rendered into more pristine English: "You can throw me in jail, but you can't give me narrower quarters than, as a seamen, I've always lived in; or a coarser food than I've always eaten, or make me lonelier than I've always been."

In the late 1890s, Mansfield and Augustus Johnson traveled to Washington on several occasions to testify with Furuseth before congressional committees. After the turn of the century, while Mansfield and Johnson concentrated on implementing the new White Bill, Furuseth teamed with Senator Robert "Fighting Bob" LaFollette to push passage of a bill that eventually became the Seamen's Act of 1915, known as the "Magna Carta of the Sea." The Seamen's Act limited working hours for most seamen to fifty-six hours a week, guaranteed minimum living standards aboard ship, abolished imprisonment for desertion, and gave seafarers the right to draw half their wages due in ports of call. In addition, the act bolstered the right of seamen to claim damages from injuries caused by the shipowner's negligence, and provided for safety—the need for which had been brought home by the sinking of the *Titanic*. The act required that vessels should have minimum lifeboat equipment, that there should be a minimum number of men employed in the deck department, and that they should be divided into equal watches.

A man of simple tastes who abhorred traditional "sailors' pleasures," Furuseth dedicated his life to the seafarers' cause and was still haunting the halls of Congress when he died at the age of eighty-four. He was buried at sea from the SS *Schoharie* on March 21, 1938, his ashes scattered "as far from land as possible," as he had wished.

---

societies would join in collective action to clean up the port were dashed. "They played the game of Conference to the extent of joining, lending the weight of their names to whatever resolutions were passed, but when it came to a matter of action or of money, they counted themselves out," Mansfield dryly commented. But Mansfield gave credit where credit was due. "With this backing, such as it was," he noted, "Mr. Johnson was able to carry out his forceful and successful campaign for cleaning up the port." And out of that campaign "grew all the practical work that the society has done; and out of the necessities of that work grew the great structure of the Institute. Hence," Mansfield concluded magnanimously, "we have reason to remember the Conference gratefully for what it did, and to lose sight of our disappointment at what it failed to do."[50]

One thing the Conference did do was help Johnson lobby Congress. On March 17, 1898, Johnson, with the full backing and blessing of the Joint Conference, went down to Washington to testify before the Senate Committee on Commerce. His mission was to push for passage of Senate Bill No. 95, the White Bill.

Discipline aboard ship. Not until the White Bill was signed into law in 1899 were flogging and all other forms of corporal punishment aboard ship abolished.

From sail to steam. The old square-rigger sailor was gradually replaced by the steamship sailor: firemen, coal passers, oilers, and marine engineers who tended the boilers and engines of the steam-driven merchant marine. Old-time tars, unimpressed, referred to these as "deckhands" and reserved the term "sailor" for windjammer men. Not until the early years of the 20th century did steam replace sail entirely as the major carrier of world commerce.

The White Bill was passed in the Senate July 2, 1898 just before Congress adjourned; the House passed it the next session, on December 12, 1898; it was signed into law on December 21 by President McKinley; and it went into effect sixty days later on February 20, 1899.

In its final form, the White Bill covered a number of topics. Seamen could demand a survey of a ship deemed unseaworthy; they were to receive compensation for discharge in case of sale of a vessel; they could demand a hearing of grievances by the American consul of a foreign port; and collect half the pay due them in any port where the vessel loaded or delivered cargo. Flogging and all other forms of corporal punishment aboard ship were abolished. Minimum daily provisions to be supplied the sailor at sea were spelled out precisely.

All well and good, and none of these important concessions stimulated much opposition by the crimps.

But the new law also abolished the payment of advance wages, and all fees for shipping seamen. Allotments to relatives or creditors (supposedly paid as earned) remained prohibited in the coastwise, or domestic, trade. In the foreign, or deep-sea, trade, though, a seaman was authorized to make any allotment he chose to a near relative and was allowed to make one to "an original creditor" not exceeding one month's wages, the latter regulation to apply to foreign ships trading in U.S. ports as well.[51]

A seaman's wages had been eighteen dollars a month in the Port of New York. The crimps, who did not care if Jack were flogged at sea or obtained decent grub, immediately organized a seafarers' strike for thirty dollars a month. The increased wage would allow the crimps to bring the one-month allotment, to which they were now limited by the law, up nearer the dollar amount they had been extracting from seafarers' advance wages and fees for shipping seamen, now abolished. The object, of course, was to make the new law unpopular with sailors. As the *New York Times* was quick to point out, by this Machiavellian maneuver the crimps quickly gained the support of their former victims. "The advantage to the sailor if he could obtain the increase was apparent. While it would enable the boarding master to get a little more out of him, it would also increase the sailor's income for a voyage."[52] The unions, usually so eager to break the power of the crimps, were unable to resist the attraction of a strike for higher wages. They, too, played into the hands of the crimps.

For Mansfield, the furor over the new law was the last straw. Up till then, he had "played the part of the peaceable parson, taking no very active part in affairs outside my parish routine, beyond keeping my eyes open and getting a correct idea of conditions in the port." But now, he fumed, "the situation stirred up all my fighting blood."[53]

Mansfield put out the word that he would do his best to help any shipowner who was against the crimp's combine, by trying to get him a crew at the old rate.

For two weeks, no American ship left port. (The strike affected only American ships; British shipping was not involved because the British Consulate still recognized the "shilling-a-month" contract.) All but two of the firms engaged in the "boarding master" business agreed to refuse to supply men for less than $30, and they swore that no ship would get a crew in this port that failed to come up to their terms.

Finally, Captain Nichols, of the shipping firm Pendleton, Carver & Nichols and a member of the Joint Conference, took Mansfield at his word. Officers for the *Emily F. Whitney* were ranging the town in the dead of night looking for crew;[54] the shipping agent, D.B. Dearborn of Beaver Street, was wringing his hands in despair, and Captain Nichols approached Mansfield for his help. A boardinghouse keeper was found who, despite the personal risk incurred by violating the crimps' embargo, was willing to provide the men — "money probably changed hands," Mansfield noted disapprovingly — and the shipping commissioner, a Major Dickey, agreed to go to the boardinghouse with Mansfield to sign the crew there so as not to have the men show themselves at Dickey's office, where they might be kidnapped by the crimps' runners.

On Friday, March 3, the *Whitney* was quietly taken from Brooklyn to an anchorage in the stream off Liberty Island. In the dead of night, when other ministers might be polishing their Sunday sermons, Mansfield, with Major Dickey in tow, was skulking through the cold, dank alleys of Sailortown to Upthur's (Negro) boardinghouse at 26 Coenties Slip, where the commissioner

The *Sentinel*. With the help of the Seamen's Benefit Society, Mansfield in 1902 purchased the launch *Sentinel* "to go about the harbor and keep watch on the malevolent activities of the crimps." It was also used to visit ships and bring seafarers to the Institute for church services and entertainments.

REAR ADMIRAL ALFRED THAYER MAHAN, U.S.N.

Rear Admiral Alfred Thayer Mahan, U.S.N. whose book *The Influence of Sea Power Upon History* made him a world-famous naval historian and naval strategist after its 1890 publication, joined the Institute's board of managers in 1867 and served for forty-seven years in various capacities. Corresponding secretary in 1897 and a lay vice president from 1898 to 1913, he took an active part in building 25 South Street. Wiry, thin, and erect, about 6'2", with finely chiseled features and a close-cropped Vandyke beard, Mahan was a familiar figure on the building committee and was greatly prized for his good humor, clear thinking, and definitive conclusions. During a time when few Americans were aware that the United States had external interests and a large number believed she ought not to have them, Mahan appointed himself "a voice to speak constantly of our external interests." The United States needed a navy with more than coastal defense capacity, he believed, challenging the popular notion of America as a nation that could live without aggression and demonstrate a new future to the world. The U.S. Navy was moribund with neglect, and in Mahan's judgment it was not a match for Chile's navy, much less Spain's.[55] "Whether they will or no," he wrote in *Atlantic Monthly* in 1893, "Americans must begin to look outward."[56]

signed twelve black men at the old wage. Mansfield then went with the men as they were marched to an unfrequented pier on the North River some distance uptown, where Captain Pendleton assembled his crew. Late the following afternoon, the sailors were picked up by a tug and taken out to the ship. The move was discovered by the crimps' patrol, who jumped into their own tugboat in hot pursuit. Both reached the ship's side at the same time. "With all their lung power the crimps tried to make the men desert, offering thirty, forty, fifty dollars spot cash to any of the twelve who would quit the *Whitney* and stick to the combine," Mansfield wrote. While none of the sailors responded, and the twelve men were passed up the side and safely stowed in the forecastle, such a ruckus ensued that Captain Pendleton, fearing that his crew might be tampered with during the night, appealed to the police, who detailed two men to stay on the ship. "All Sunday night the police stood watch on the decks of the *Whitney*," the *New York Times* reported, "while at intervals the tug containing the boardinghouse keepers came near enough to fire a broadside of promises at the men. They stayed by the ship, however, and early [Monday] morning the *Whitney* sailed for Honolulu."

Ominously, the *Times* added, "Both sides say they are going to fight it out if it takes all Summer."[57]

They did fight it out. A week after the *Whitney* sailed, the *John R. Kelly* became the first ship to take a crew at the $30 rate.[58] At the same time, Mansfield and the commissioner, Major Dickey, secretly signed a black crew of twelve at a Baxter Street boardinghouse and got them aboard — via one of the Dalzell

SEAMEN'S CHURCH INSTITUTE

Towing the second Floating Church of Our Saviour. Built in 1869 to replace its namesake, which had been declared unseaworthy, the third and last of these nautical chapels operated by the Society remained in use until 1910. On January 6, 1911, the church was towed to Mariner's Harbor, Staten Island, where it was moved ashore and became All Saints Episcopal Church. It served its congregation until 1958, when it burned to the ground the day after Christmas.

tugboats, escorted by a police launch — the American bark *Francis S. Hampshire*, without trouble.[59] Between May 5 and 12, Mansfield lined up nineteen men for Captain Nichols; seventeen were kidnapped by crimps on their way to the vessels, and the *Mary R. Cushing*, *State of Maine*, and *Benjamin F. Packard* laid off Staten Island for days, unable to get crew.[60]

Finally, "the Joint Conference woke up from its long sleep," in Mansfield's words, "and held a meeting — its last one, with Mr. Johnson in the chair." The meeting, on May 12, 1899, at the American Seamen's Friend Society at 76 Wall Street, was attended by representatives of the New York Port Society, Mariners' Society, and the American Seamen's Friend Society, and was covered by the *New York Times*; Mansfield was getting the publicity he wanted. "Resolutions were passed deploring the inefficiency of the United States District Attorney's Office in New York in securing and presenting evidence in supports of claims and complaints made on behalf of seamen," the reporter wrote the next day, "and demanding that all boarding house keepers, shipping masters, and runners who have violated the law be prosecuted." Also demanded: that the State Board for Licensing Sailors' Hotels revoke the licenses of boardinghouse keepers who had "entered combinations to prevent the shipping of crews"; and that the police put on board every incoming sailing vessel an officer "in order to protect its crew against runners for boarding houses, and prevent all unlawful boarding by other persons."[61]

Copies of the resolution were sent to everyone even remotely interested in the plight of seamen, from the President of the United States and the attorney general on down to the mayor and police commissioner of New York; a copy was even sent to the British Board of Trade in England.

By measures such as this — personally signing seafarers in the dead of night, hammering away at problems in every practical sense of the word, pushing through federal and state legislation and demanding that that legislation be enforced, constantly keeping the plight of the seafarer before the eyes of the public — Mansfield and Johnson and the Society were able to accomplish their goal: amelioration of the condition of seamen in the Port of New York and beyond.

It took longer than the summer of 1899. Crimping would not totally die out until the 1930s.

But Mansfield won the war.

Soon he was in a position to "do for the sailor's good exactly what the crimps had been doing for his harm."

Now all he needed was a new building in which to do it.

J. Augustus Johnson was the first to articulate the vision: a building that would house the various branches of the work, he said wistfully in 1902. If possible, it would afford space for other not-for-profit societies. A building facing Battery Park that would cover two lots would be from six to eight stories high, and would accommodate 250 beds. On the ground floor there should be a free shipping bureau, a large supply store with all sailors' furnishings at a reasonable price, and a Seamen's Branch of the Legal Aid Society. The building should have a high tower with an illuminated clock and a Star of Hope.

And all this should be under the charge of a paid superintendent and a paid secretary, who should look after national and state legislation and the general interests of sailors in American and foreign lands.[62]

And the Society would need a new name, Mansfield put in; "The Protestant Episcopal Church Missionary Society for Seamen in the City and Port of New York" was *way* too long. Something snappier was needed: "A policy-announcing phrase," Mansfield thought, might fit the bill nicely.

Mansfield tells us how the name change came about:

Captain (afterwards Admiral) Alfred T. Mahan said, "Let us get at it this way. Who is it we are working for?" We all said, "Seamen." "All right, put that down. Now under what auspices are we working? What is back of us?" We said, "The Church." "All right, put that down — Church. Now what kind of work are we doing?" "Institutional work." "Very well, put that down. Institute. Seamen's Church Institute — there we have it, I think."[63]

In 1906, the New York legislature passed a bill permitting the name change to Seamen's Church Institute of New York.

So they had the new name; now all they needed was the new building — and a few big personalities to get the project off the ground.

One of these was Edmund Lincoln Baylies, a member of the board of managers since 1886 and its president from 1913 until his death in 1932. Large in physique and in personality, Baylies "planned things in a big way," a former staff member of the Institute has written, "and never permitted the factor of cost

THE *TITANIC* MEMORIAL LIGHTHOUSE

The *Titanic* Memorial

A service commemorating the anniversary of the sinking of the *Titanic*

"In the gloom of a rainy evening, as the Staten Island ferry-boat creeps on through mist to its slip on the south tip of Manhattan Island, the veil ahead is suddenly pierced as if by a huge green eye. Glowing in pure aquamarine, like an enormous jewel, it points the way until the gray veil lifts... the deep phosphorescent glow of the *Titanic* Memorial — a symbol of safety and a monument to sentiment." Thus *Harper's* described the lighthouse in 1915.[64] Rising 216 feet above the waters of the East River and displaying a green light visible to ships anywhere in the Upper Bay — a range of twelve miles — the lighthouse structure on the roof of 25 South Street soon became a navigation aid and appeared on nautical charts until 1968, when the building was torn down to make way for a new office tower at 55 Water Street. Friends of South Street Seaport Museum then acquired the lighthouse, and, with funds from Exxon Corporation, in May 1976 installed it on a specially built concrete tower at the corner of Fulton and Water Streets.

HEROES OF THE TITANIC

HONOR THE BRAVE WHO SLEEP
WHERE THE LOST TITANIC LIES.
THE MEN WHO KNEW WHAT A MAN MUST DO
WHEN HE LOOKS DEATH IN THE EYES.

"WOMEN AND CHILDREN FIRST"
OH, STRONG AND TENDER CRY.
THE SONS WHOM WOMEN HAD BORNE AND NURSED
REMEMBERED - AND DARED TO DIE.

THE BOATS CREPT OFF IN THE DARK
THE GREAT SHIP GROANED - AND THEN -
O STARS OF THE NIGHT WHO SAW THAT SIGHT
BEAR WITNESS THESE WERE MEN!

HENRY VAN DYKE

Commemorative plaque

to prevent carrying his plans into execution. . . . He and Mansfield were fitly joined together. Both were large planners and free spenders. Both had one motivating motto, 'Nothing is too good for seamen.'"[65]

First, consolidation was in order. In 1906, 34 Pike Street and the Sailors' Home at 52 Market Street were sold and the cash from these transactions put into the Building Fund. Next Mansfield convinced the Episcopal Diocese in Brooklyn to become financially responsible for the Breakwater in Brooklyn, enabling the Seamen's Church Institute to withdraw from that borough. In 1908, the American Seamen's Friend Society opened the Sailors' Home and Institute opposite Pier 51 on the North River. It had a restaurant; more than two hundred rooms; a chapel; billiards, pool; and other indoor games; a swimming pool, and a concert hall. Mansfield accordingly decided that the ASFS had provided nicely for the needs of seamen whose ships docked in the North River, and he made plans to close the North River Branch of the Institute as soon as arrangements could be made for the staff there.

In 1906, the building committee had acquired a site of ninety square feet at South Street and Coenties Slip, where the original Coenties Slip Station had been located; by 1912, the committee under Baylies's able chairmanship was ready to begin construction. The cornerstone of the Seamen's Church Institute was laid on Tuesday, April 15, 1912, by the mayor of New York, the Honorable William Jay Gaynor. But the festivity of the occasion was marred by an appalling marine disaster the day before — the sinking of the White Star Liner *Titanic* on her maiden voyage with a loss of 1,600 lives. The *Titanic* Memorial Lighthouse, atop the new building, was dedicated a year later, on April 15, 1913.

Mansfield was in his element as a builder. During the long, hot summer of 1900, the twenty-nine-year-old chaplain had become so passionately involved in supervising the renovation of the Society's Pike Street Mission House that he had exhausted himself and had almost died of pleurisy. In 1912, a more mature Mansfield managed to avoid life-threatening illness; still, he said on one occasion that "looking back upon the erection of the Institute it seemed as if he had seen every shovelful of earth removed, every brick and stone laid, every screw driven and every piece of mechanism set up in its place."[66]

The new Institute at 25 South Street was formally opened on May 28, 1913. "A thick sea fog hung low over the city all day and it poured heavily at intervals," Katharine Lane Spaeth, the editor of *The Lookout*, reported. "But a little water could hardly be expected to interfere with the opening of an institution dedicated to seafaring men." Flags were hoisted on the roof: the American flag, the blue flag of the Institute with the Institute's seal in white and red; and three code flags spelling "Welcome." The ladies of the Seamen's Benefit Society served tea in the Apprentice Room. Everyone was giddy with accomplishment. The following September, Spaeth exuberantly wrote:

> On Monday September 15th the first seaman can enter the building as a lodger. He can get his key from the keyboard at the Hotel Desk, take the elevator to his room and go to sleep that night secure in the conviction that he will neither be aroused by a drunken quarrel nor be robbed in the darkness.

SEAMEN'S CHURCH INSTITUTE

Although it will not be possible to open the Dining Rooms and Lunch Counter until after the $195,000 still needed has been subscribed, it was thought best to put in use the empty rooms which stand ready for the seamen guests.

Notices of the opening of this part of the Institute will be sent all over the world, together with pictures of the new building. When a sailor is leaving an Institute in Hong Kong he will have the address of No. 25 South Street, New York. He will enter this port with the knowledge that he is to be welcomed, to be treated with consideration. He will know that a clean bed in attractive surroundings awaits him; that his luggage will be cared for, his mail received for him; that he will find amusement; that — and perhaps this will be the best part of what he realizes instinctively — he will be living in a place where people care about him as an individual, where people want him to be happy.[67]

To make the seamen feel comfortable bringing their mothers, sisters, and sweethearts to the Institute, Mansfield appointed "women of culture" to various positions in the social and recreation rooms. "Mansfield employed women who could have filled acceptably important positions in the best places of business in the City," wrote the Reverend James C. Healey, looking back on his arrival to take up duties at the Institute in 1915. "For the most part they were young, were college trained, came from good families and had poise which enabled them to greet seamen without flutter."[68] The appointment of women to staff positions at the Institute was considered an astonishing modernization, all the more appreciated, Healey pointed out, since at the time "the United States Marine Hospitals had no female nurses and no Social Service Auxiliary staffed by women. The seaman worked, had his recreation and his sickness in a masculine environment. Mansfield changed the atmosphere of the waterfront by this startling innovation."[69]

The hotel part of the new building accommodated 580 men. Dormitory beds were fifteen cents a night, rooms twenty-five cents, and ninety men took lodgings on the first night. On October 12, the Chapel of Our Saviour was dedicated by Bishop Greer, and, at long last, it could be said that the building that Johnson, Mansfield, Baylies, and other members of the board had envisioned and planned was truly launched: a building in which Mansfield could run a hotel, manage a shipping bureau, operate a restaurant, and furnish postal and dunnage services.

The Reverend Archibald Romaine Mansfield, at the age of forty-two and in his seventeenth year of service to the Seamen's Church Institute, had realized a dream.

25 South Street
under construction

SEAMEN OF THE MERCHANT MARINE,
THE MEN OF THE HOUR.
SEAMENS CHURCH INSTITUTE OF NEW YORK 25 SOUT

CHAPTER THREE

The Seamen's Church Institute Goes to War

"Read all about it," shouted the newsboys on the afternoon of June 3, 1918. "Nine ships sunk off American shores!"

A Seamen's Church Institute chaplain, returning to his office in the Institute when he heard the news, was as incredulous as the rest of the country. Enemy submarines, *here*? Operating in American coastal waters? Not since the War of 1812 had enemy fighting craft invaded American waters. Another device to sell extras, he scoffed. He did not even stop to buy a paper, but continued on his way.

In June 1918, Europe was beginning its fifth bitter summer at war. The United States had declared war on Germany on April 6, 1917, but despite the participation of American Expeditionary Forces in the fighting, for most Americans it was "the European war," something that was taking place "over there."

At the Institute, which by this time had a reputation for running an operation patronized almost entirely by foreigners, the war seemed closer. Indeed, since August 1914, when SCI staffers waved goodbye to their beloved apprentice lads — boys of fourteen or fifteen years of age in the British merchant marine, who went home to England to find places in the army — the Institute had been, in a sense, at war. The immediate effect of the European war upon seafarers was unemployment. Ships that had sailed under flags of the now-belligerent nations languished in New York Harbor while their owners scrambled to complete the paperwork to put themselves under the neutral American flag; colliers bound for Central and South America canceled sailings after reports of German warships lying in wait off the shores of Venezuela and Brazil, eager to capture neutral coal cargo; German liners such as the 54,000-ton *Vaterland* dared not sail for fear of capture by the British. Seafarers who would have crewed on these vessels were suddenly out of work — and turning up on the Institute's doorstep. Before long,

Seamen of the merchant marine: the "men of the hour" during World War I

A rescued crew from a torpedoed vessel. These seafarers were among the lucky ones. In August, 1917, the editor of The Lookout *grimly noted that "probably 100,000 merchant mariners of all nations have been drowned or killed some way since the war began."*[70]

the Institute's savings programs for seamen were disrupted; the United States Post Office abruptly announced it would not guarantee international money orders payable in any European country "until after the restoration of peace and normal conditions."

Soon the war hit home even more directly: On May 7, 1915, the *Lusitania* was torpedoed ten miles off Old Head, Kinsale, on the southeast tip of Ireland, with a loss of 1,198 noncombatants, including 124 Americans. Among them were a number of seafarers known at the Institute, as well as Alfred G. Vanderbilt, who had given $10,000 for the new SCI building. (Also aboard was Charles W. Bowring of the board of managers, who laconically cabled, "Torpedoed without warning, port side; overboard starboard side; in water four hours; no ill effects.")

In February 1916, six British ships were sunk by the German surface raider *Möwe* off the coasts of Spain and Africa. The crews, picked up by westbound merchantmen, landed in Norfolk, Virginia, and were taken to 25 South Street, to be sheltered at SCI until the British Consulate could send them back to England aboard other ships. A near-crisis in logistics ensued when another 134 men, from the steamers *Author, Trader, Ariadne, Corbridge, Farringford, Dummonby,* and *Appam,* were landed in New York and taken to the Institute; cots and blankets were borrowed from the Naval Branch YMCA; clothes were hustled up for those who needed them; and an entertainment program was quickly organized for the men during their stay. On March 18, 1916, the British freighter *Trevose* was torpedoed. Most of her crew was picked up by another British freighter, *Alnwick Castle,* which was herself torpedoed and sunk the very next day. Seven men in one of the lifeboats froze to death before the SS *Venezia* arrived on the scene, picked up the survivors, and brought them to New York and the Institute.

Finally, after the sinking of the French channel steamer *Sussex*, a passenger liner carrying civilians from England to France, in May 1916, President Wilson threatened to break relations with Germany unless Germany pledged not to renew attacks on merchant ships without warning. Germany grudgingly offered a conditioned pledge, and between May 4, 1916 and January 31, 1917 there were no sinkings of merchantmen.

It was an uneasy truce, and it did not last. On February 1, 1917, the Germans resumed unrestricted submarine warfare. And on April 2, 1917, Wilson, declaring that "the world must be made safe for democracy," urged Congress and the American people to "formally accept the status of belligerent." America must fight "for the principles that gave her birth," Wilson declared. "God help her, she can do no other."[71] All in all, four U.S. vessels had been sunk before the *Lusitania*; nine were sunk after the *Lusitania* up until the declaration of war. Many Americans went down with British, French, and Italian ships.

Still, amazingly, the war was "over there." The shouting of the newsboys on the afternoon of June 3, 1918, was the first inkling most Americans would have that the war was now over here.

Captain C.E. Holbrook and his crew were unlucky enough to get their inkling almost two weeks earlier; for them, the war ceased to be "over there" on the morning of May 25. Aboard the three-masted American schooner *Hattie Dunn*, they were en route in ballast from New York to Charleston, South Carolina, when, about twenty miles off Winter Quarter Lightship, Delaware, the Imperial German submarine SM *Unterseeboot-151*, captained by *Korvettenkapitan*

The *Lusitania*. Torpedoed on May 7, 1915, off the southeast coast of Ireland, the ship went down with a loss of 1,198 noncombatants, including 124 Americans.

British apprentice lads at a festive dinner in the Institute's Apprentice Room

(Lieutenant Commander) von Nostitz und Janckendorf, surfaced from the deep and fired a shot across *Hattie Dunn*'s bow. Captain Holbrook, mistaking the *U-151* for an American submarine, paid no attention; when a second shot fell astern, Holbrook simply adjusted his course to get out of range. A third shot over the bow forced him to heave to. Taken prisoner by the Germans, Captain Holbrook and his crew of seven were ordered below decks on the submarine. The schooner was blown up with bombs.

Five miles away, the crew of the new four-masted steel schooner *Hauppauge* heard the shelling of the *Hattie Dunn*. Not until they actually laid eyes on the German submarine, however, did they consider the possibility they might come under attack. The first shot fell short; the second ripped through the ship's side about five feet above the waterline. Captain Sweeney, master of the *Hauppauge*, ordered the ship hove to. Soon he and his crew of eleven were prisoners aboard the *U-151*. At 11:30 A.M. bombs placed aboard the schooner by the German seamen exploded, sending a shower of debris sky high. The *Hauppauge* slowly rolled over on her beam ends but continued to float.

Aboard the *U-151*, Commander von Nostitz politely gave the bemused Captains Holbrook and Sweeney receipts for their bombed vessels.

In no time, another three-master was sighted on the horizon, approaching with all sails set. It was the *Edna*, bound from Philadelphia to Santiago with a cargo of oil and gasoline. Firing had been heard by the crew of the *Edna*, but they had taken it for American naval vessels at target practice. At 1:30 P.M. a shell whistled overhead as the *U-151* approached, flying the German war ensign. Captain C.W. Gilmore ran up the American ensign, lowered his jibs, and hove to. Two German officers and four men climbed over the railing and cordially shook hands with the *Edna*'s crew. By 2 P.M. they were below decks on the submarine; once again the bombs exploded, and the *Edna* was left in a sinking condition.

The six members of the *Edna*'s crew swelled the prisoner list on the U-boat to twenty-six. The crew of the *Hattie Dunn* were all elderly men; the crew of the *Hauppauge* were young Danes and Norwegians; and the *Edna*'s crew, except for the captain and one Portuguese sailor, were African-American. Captain Holbrook of the *Hauppauge* and Captain Gilmore of the *Edna* had something of a reunion; boyhood friends in the village of St. George, Maine, they had not seen each other in more than thirty years. Their hilarity over seeing one another after so many years under such ludicrous circumstances spread even to the Germans, who entered into the spirit of reunion and passed out cognac.

Meanwhile, on the surface, the *Mohawk*, a Clyde Line passenger liner bound from Jacksonville to New York, passed the partly submerged wrecks of the *Hattie Dunn* and *Hauppauge*; barely half an hour after that, the third derelict, the *Edna*, hove into view, her decks awash. When a boarding party determined no one was aboard, the *Mohawk*'s captain, disquieted, decided to tow the *Edna* to Port Richmond, where she was examined by officers from the Fourth Naval District. It was hard to miss the two jagged holes in her bottom two to three feet across. Likewise the damaged time fuse, the first visible evidence of enemy submarines off the American coast.

The Navy Department, confronted with this evidence, chose to censor it. The British Admiralty had alerted the Navy weeks earlier that a German submarine of the *Deutschland* class would soon arrive in American waters. There were circumstances, however, the Brits cautioned, that rendered it "highly important that nothing whatsoever should be given out which would lead the enemy even to surmise that we had any advance information concerning this submarine."[72] Despite news stories prompted by the reports of the crew and passengers of the *Mohawk*, the Navy Department released an oblique statement

The *J. Hooker Hamersley*. Presented to the Institute in 1915 by Louis Gordon Hamersley in memory of his father, the tender carried crews and dunnage to and from ships. During the war it was also used as a training vessel by SCI's maritime training school, and for evening picnic excursions to Coney Island — often offering roller-coaster rides to seafarers who were last afloat in a lifeboat.

A postcard written in 1917 by Paddy Smith, a British apprentice staying at the Institute, to his mother in England

on May 28 declaring that derelicts off the Virginia Capes had given rise to "rumors" that German submarines or raiders had been operating along the coast recently. Not so, insisted the Navy. The derelict was merely the wreck of a coastal schooner that had crashed into another off Winter Quarter Shoals, Delaware, the previous week.[73]

Demands from the public and the press for information became more insistent, but each day the Navy calmly reported that it was "standing by" for further developments. It stood by until the *U-151* emerged from concealment, dramatically and suddenly, early Sunday morning, June 2, 1918. Capturing in quick succession the American schooner *Isabel B. Wiley* and the American steamer *Winneconne* — whose chief officer mistook the submarine for an American patrol boat, until a shell whistled by — Commander von Nostitz released his twenty-six prisoners from the *Hattie Dunn*, *Hauppauge*, and *Edna* and divided them among the two lifeboats from the *Winneconne* and a motor launch and lifeboat from the *Isabel B. Wiley*. When the lifeboats were safely away, the *Winneconne* and *Wiley* were blown up with bombs placed aboard.

By the end of the day, the *U-151* had registered nine successful attacks upon unarmed vessels (including the *Hattie Dunn*, *Hauppauge*, and *Edna*); in addition to the *Wiley* and the *Winneconne*, Commander von Nostitz and his men sank the *Jacob M. Haskell*, the *Edward Cole*, the *Texel*, and the passenger liner *Carolina*. During the course of this one day, 448 persons were set adrift in lifeboats.

At 5:37 A.M. Monday morning, June 3, 1918, the first survivors reached New York: eleven crew from the *Edward Cole*, picked up shortly after being set adrift. That morning the airwaves began to crackle with reports of sinkings, submarine warnings, false rumors, and dire speculation. Later in the day, a second group arrived at the Battery, including members of the crews that had been held prisoner aboard the German U-boat, who amazed all hearers with their tales of good food and good treatment, cognac, and fraternization with the German submarine crew — most of whom spoke excellent English — and above all the colorful Commander von Nostitz. The same day, two lifeboats from the *Texel*, after thirty-six hours of continued rowing, landed in Atlantic City. Also landing in Atlantic City — smack in the middle of a boardwalk parade of Shriners, who rushed onto the beach to aid the people staggering ashore — was one lifeboat of six from the *Carolina*.

The chaplain from the Seamen's Church Institute, after scoffing at the newsboys, arrived that same Monday afternoon back at his office, where, to his surprise, the news was confirmed by the ticker and telephone calls from various sources.

The following account is taken from the June 1918 *Lookout*:

> Some of those crews will be coming here," [the chaplain] told the staff, and at eight o'clock the Naval Intelligence office called up to say that the crews were arriving in New York and would need the shelter of 25 South Street.... There were only 30 available beds in the building, but cots were quickly set up, all arrangements made, and everything kept open, waiting. The Soda Fountain was surrounded by jostling, excited seamen, keeping one eye on their glasses of iced syrups and one upon the Main Entrance through which the shipwrecked crews would presently make their way. The Lunch Counter did not put away its sandwiches, or empty its shining coffee urns, and the waiters did not fold up their white aprons at the usual hour. Everyone was waiting, restlessly anxious to see the heroes of the latest war adventure, and to hear how things had happened....
>
> Up in Dr. Mansfield's office the telephone rang steadily. First it would be reporters asking for news, then the government officials requesting that the crews give out no news to reporters; then an order from the Old Slip Police Station saying that their policemen should be allowed to come over and protect the men as they arrived. The government specially requested that the submarine sinkings should be given as little publicity as possible.
>
> Out on the sidewalk were groups of restless photographers and newspaper men, seething back and forth, fearful lest a fluttering wing of a story should escape them.
>
> At last one man came, escorted by a Naval Reserve man. He was surrounded by clamoring reporters, but his mouth was closed; he glanced at them with friendly eyes, not at all unwilling to figure on the printed page, but the Naval Reserve guardian was stern, and the seaman went into the Institute. For hours they kept coming, one at a time, after making their statements at the Customs House. It was three in the morning before the last one got to bed.

As the June 1918 *Lookout* went to press, the Institute had lodged most of the crews from the SS *Winneconne*, schooner *Edna*, schooner *Hattie Dunn*, SS *Carolina*, SS *Texel*, SS *Hauppauge*, schooner *Samuel C. Mengel*, and schooner *Isabel B. Wiley*. "The war is closer down here," Katharine Lane Spaeth, the editor of *The Lookout*, commented afterward, "closer even than it is on Fifth Avenue, when the men in uniforms march and flags float above their heads and the bands play."

The *U-151* was the first of six German subs sent to American coastal waters in the summer of 1918. Commanders of those that followed were less sportsmanlike than the gentlemanly von Nostitz. Altogether, the six submarines sank ninety-one vessels, half of which were American, and took 368 lives in the process.[74]

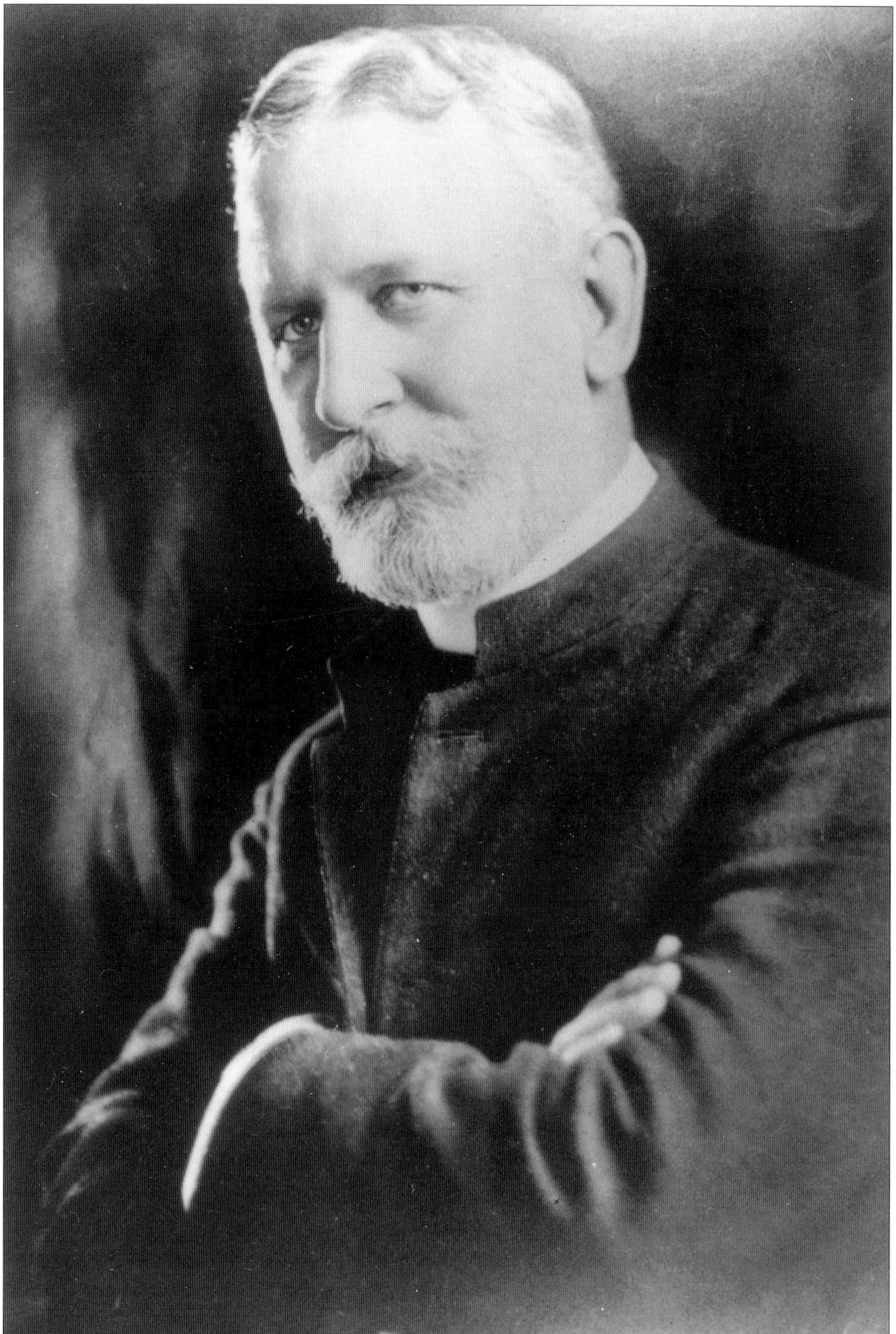

CHAPTER FOUR

Mansfield's Dream Hotel

The Annual Report for 1919 noted that the Seamen's Church Institute at 25 South Street had 240 employees to carry out "the exceedingly practical work in this Port." *Practical* was the key word. There followed a report on the operation of the building, with its beds for 714 seamen ("but not beds for all who come; the House is generally booked before noon"); the concierge-type activities of the hotel desk; the handling of seamen's mail and dunnage; and the banking of their money on their behalf.

Only after cataloguing these laudable enterprises did the report mention anything remotely "religious" in nature; even then, the "religious work" was lumped together with the other work carried on by the Institute's Religious and Social Work Department: the relief work, the loan fund, the Lost and Found Department, the Department of Missing Men, the reading and writing rooms, the medical relief, and recreation.

The seafarers themselves thought "practical" first and "church" second — or third, or fourth. In the mid-1920s, a sixteen-year-old boy, looking for a ship, got this rundown of the Institute from a kindly old salt: "You can eat there; sleep there; they'll stow your gear. It's cheap and it's clean. They got a job board — tell you what ships are lookin' for a crew. They got it all; and they ain't *too* holy."[75]

Nor were the Institute staffers sentimental about the men they cared for. Mansfield's no-nonsense practicality led him to hire earthy but creative people to staff his dream hotel for seafarers at 25 South Street. House Mother Janet Roper, who arrived at the Institute in 1915, brought to her job twenty-five years of experience working with seafarers and an ingenuity of Solomonic proportions. The Reverend Carl Podin, a Latvian by birth, spoke half a dozen Slavic languages, including Russian; Mansfield hired him not because of his linguistic abilities, however, but because he had seen Podin waltzing up and down the street in front of the Seamen's Mission in Brooklyn, playing a violin to attract

Archibald R. Mansfield

47

sailors to a chapel service.[76] The Reverend J.G. Robinson, who took up supervision of the religious work in 1918, was considered uniquely qualified for the post of chaplain — because he had an "unshockable mind."[77]

Perhaps the most bald-eyed of the early employees of "Twenty-five," as Mansfield's hotel-*cum*-social-services outfit soon came to be known, was Katharine Lane Spaeth (formerly Irene Katharine Lane), first editor of *The Lookout*, a post she held from 1911 through October 1919. Spaeth considered it part of her job to dispel superstitions and romantic notions about mariners. "They're far from the rough rascals of the lubber's imagination," she said in an interview in 1915. "They work hard and send most of their money home . . . . [In fact] there is no other class of men who send so much of their earnings home to relatives, despite the tradition that the deep-sea sailor is an irresponsible rover."[78] On the other hand, Spaeth was willing to call a spade a spade. It was she who devised the "psychological" soda fountain with the brass rail in the Institute's foyer, exactly like the bar in a saloon, with the exception that it served no alcoholic drinks. And in May 1916, Spaeth had written this blunt assessment of seafarers seeking financial aid from the Institute:

> The man who asks for aid can come under any one of ten heads. He may have been ill; he may have been injured on board his last boat; he may have been robbed; he may have been beaten by the thugs who robbed him; he may have been drugged in a saloon; he may have spent all his money on drink; he may have spent his money carelessly without realizing how inevitably it was disappearing; he may have lost his money through torn pockets; he may have lent too generously to his friends; he may have missed his boat through some misunderstanding of the city and its piers. Or he may simply think that the Institute is supposed to take care of careless, irresponsible seamen. . . .
>
> "That sign up there says, 'This Institute is willing to help men' and that is what you are here for," argues the applicant.
>
> "The sign reads, 'This Institute is willing to help men help themselves,'" finishes the Relief Man crisply.

While pointing out that "the fine line between charity and philanthropy is a very delicate one," Spaeth was quick to reassure *The Lookout* readers that the majority of seamen were "an intensely self-respecting lot" who did not "ask nor expect favors any more than most of us ask or expect favors of the management when we are staying at hotels."

During the First World War — and the following two decades — philanthropy as it was practiced at "The House That Built Jack" (as the Institute liked to call itself) was undertaken in a spirit of benevolent paternalism that might not pass today's standards of political correctness. Yet it was appropriate in its time, especially given the fact that most of the recipients of the philanthropy were boys under twenty, far from hearth and home, who benefitted enormously from "a kind of institutional mother," as the *New York Post* would describe SCI in 1930.[79] Mansfield's hotel, with its post office and lunch counter, medical clinic and social work office, laundry and bathing facilities, its Navigation and Marine Engineering School and its Savings Department — and, yes, its chapel — was

Edmund Lincoln Baylies

First elected to the board of managers in 1885, Baylies, an admiralty lawyer, served as a member of J. Augustus Johnson's important committee on legislation, and later as the Institute's attorney. In 1905, he was chosen as the first lay president of the Institute, and he continued in this capacity until 1932. At his death that year, he had been a member of the Board for forty-six years.

It was Baylies who chose the site for 25 South Street, purchased some five separate plots of land for it, and interested the architectural firm of Whitney Warren and Charles Wetmore in drawing up plans for a "reproduction on a large scale of the old type of Dutch warehouse" he had in mind.[80] Baylies also supervised the construction of the Institute Annex in the 1920s. Perhaps his greatest contribution to SCI was his inspired fund-raising. He encouraged a spirited rivalry between J.P. Morgan and John D. Rockefeller, one result of which was this 1923 headline in the *New York Evening Mail*: "Seamen's Institute in New York Example of How Multimillionaires Vie in Charity Work: J.P. Morgan gave 25,000 Toward Erection of 1,250,000 Building; Came Back With 50,000 More When J.D. Rockefeller Gave 50,000—Proves Real Home for Sailors."[81]

---

a veritable paradigm of institutional church work and a model for present and future social work among seafarers.

At the General Convention of the Episcopal Church in St. Louis in 1916, a national organization of seamen's missions was finally pulled together, after a number of false starts. Called the Seamen's Church Institute of America to distinguish it from its prototype in New York, the new organization elected a number of temporary, organizing officers and threw itself immediately into war work. On June 1, 1916, Dr. Mansfield dispatched his righthand man, assistant superintendent Charles P. Deems (on more than one occasion *The Lookout*'s Man Who Gives Advice), to California, to take over the San Francisco branch of the English Mission to Seamen and reorganize it into an institute similar to the Seamen's Church Institute in New York. On June 10, 1920, the Seamen's Church Institute of America was legally incorporated; among its many permanent officers now elected were Edmund L. Baylies, president, and Dr. Mansfield, general superintendent. Soon *The Lookout* began to report on the activities of nascent institutes inspired by the New York operation: groups in New Orleans, Philadelphia; Norfolk, Virginia; Newport, Rhode Island; Port Arthur, Texas and other ports were staking out claims along the wharves, raising new buildings for new enterprises.

Back in New York, life at 25 South Street bustled on. Dormitory beds were fifteen cents a night; rooms, twenty-five cents. Shower facilities included a sink where a sailor could wash his clothes; he could then hang them in a "drying closet" while he himself bathed, emerging half an hour later a new man. The lunch counter dispensed wholesome food in wholesome portions at reasonable prices, and the soda fountain advertised non-alcoholic drinks in fifteen languages, including Chinese. Free stationery was available in the writing room. The reading room was stocked with foreign newspapers and magazines, including *Punch*, a favorite of the British apprentice lads. The Institute tenders, the *J. Hooker Hamersley* and the *Brown Betty*, offered free transportation to and from ships anchored out, and the Free Shipping Bureau would find a man a berth at no cost. Also on the Institute premises was the British Consular Shipping Office, where the seamen employed on British vessels were engaged and paid off.[82]

The Institute encouraged seafarers to deposit their money in Twenty-five's

25 South Street

Savings Department. Frequently called the Institute's "bank," the Savings Department did not actually function in the strictest banking sense; it had no charter, paid no interest, and its purpose in taking the sailor's money was purely for safekeeping. When amounts of a fair size had been deposited, the depositor was advised to put his money in a chartered, interest-paying bank. The Institute would deposit his money for him, if he wished, with the Seamen's Bank for Savings, the Union Square Savings Bank, or the Immigrant Savings Bank. The Institute also made arrangements for seafarers to "Send money home to Mom", wherever Mom might be; sailors, with the Institute's help, sent international money orders all around the world. Soon seamen from the rank of messboy to captain were lining up to deposit their hard-earned cash in the Institute's coffers. But old ways died hard. "I *do* wish they'd stop saving in their shoes," William E. Bunce, cashier for twelve years at 25 South Street, would grumble as late as 1930. "I resent the way they come in here and disrobe their feet before my window all day long."[83]

Down in the bowels of 25 South Street, which extended three stories below ground, was located the Baggage Department, where a man could check his "dunnage" — the seafaring term for baggage — while ashore or at sea. This service had become especially popular during World War I, when men frequently lost all their possessions due to torpedoings. "Experience with submarines has taught them that they are certain to lose their luggage, even if they save their lives," Spaeth noted in May 1918, "and the wise sailor who has letters and photographs and small belongings which he prizes, has packed them in a bag or suitcase and checked them in the Institute Baggage Room." In December 1921, the editor of *The Lookout* reported that more than 80,000 pieces of luggage had been checked during the previous year.

Formerly a sailor had had no "real" address, spending his time ashore in whatever boardinghouse had managed to get its runners aboard his ship first when it anchored. Mansfield determined to give the seafaring man a Home with a capital "H." It was not long before a local newspaper reported that "25 South Street is the most popular address in the world." It was often the only stable address a seagoing man had. The Institute Post Office, which by 1921 was handling as much mail as the post office of a city of 15,000, received mail from all over the world, some of it in foreign languages or near-illegible handwriting. Missives arrived in care of "Sailors, South Street, N.Y."; "Sailors Home with the green light, New York"; or "Sailors' Home near South Ferry, New York"; among others. The Institute Post Office clerks sorted through it all; they would hold mail for a year, or forward it anywhere requested. In 1927, the mail operation reached a size equal to that of a post office in a city of 20,000, and Mansfield decided it had become too unwieldy for the Institute to continue to manage. He struck a deal with the U.S. Post Office. Uncle Sam agreed to rent the space for a dollar a year, take charge of the seafarers' mail, and establish a branch U.S. Post Office — the Seamen's Institute Station — at 25 South Street.

Entertainment had become a large part of the program at SCI New York,

SEAMEN'S CHURCH INSTITUTE

The Post Office at 25 South Street

The soda fountain and luncheonette

The tailor shop

mainly because Institute staffers still worried that seamen abroad in the wee hours might very well be robbed, rolled, or beaten, or have their drinks doctored with knockout drops. Shanghaiing still occurred, although less frequently than it had in the days before Mansfield and his allies cleaned up the port, and there were sharks out there, the ones in human form. During Prohibition (1920–1933), a man could be blinded, crazed, or poisoned in the "blind tigers" and speakeasies by bad moonshine. (The Broad Street Hospital just up the street from the Institute was kept busy during the "dry" years pumping out the stomachs of sailors laid low by Bowery "smoke," a murderous distillation concocted by burning part of the poison out of wood alcohol with a red-hot poker.) Consequently, the chaplains protectively sought to keep the seafarers "at home" at 25 South Street.

Good inducements to stay home were the slide shows, musicales, songfests, and other evening entertainments arranged by the staff and volunteers. "When three or four hundred men come to the Concert Hall from eight to nine-thirty, they are not likely to want to go out upon the waterfront afterward, hunting for something less innocuous by way of diversion," one staff member explained, perhaps naively, in 1918.[84] The motion-picture evenings were enormously popular; the silent movies required no command of English and could be shown to a room full of Norwegians, Danes, Egyptians, Frenchmen, Lascars [East Indians], and Spaniards. Roller-skating was another success, also requiring no common language. "Rollers against gloom and worry and harassed minds," the staffers enthused. Besides which, as one wag noted, "If we could let them roller skate every evening, it is unlikely that they would ever crave the rolling induced by over-cheering liquids."[85]

One of the most far-reaching of the Institute's services to seafarers came in September 1919, when House Mother Janet Roper and her co-workers in the Religious and Social Work Department established a Missing Men Department. Its goal was "to encircle the world with a band of men and women who care enough for seamen to help them to keep in touch with their families and friends," as Spaeth put it.[86] Roper began to issue a weekly newsletter, the *Missing Seamen Bulletin*, which she mailed to hundreds of institutes, missions, union halls, marine hospitals, consulates, and shipping commissioners around the world. Soon responses began to arrive from faraway ports such as Rotterdam, Buenos Aires, Honolulu, Shanghai, and Singapore. A "missing" seaman, having seen his name in the bulletin, might write asking who wanted him and why; another might send word that he had seen in the bulletin the name of a pal swept overboard in a storm. But for the most part the missing were those who in their voyages about the earth had lost their "connections."[87] As the *New York Sun* put it:

> Seamen are forever getting lost. Not lost in the intricate streets of a foreign city, but lost from their families somewhere out in the wide world. Sometimes their lost state is deliberate, but often it is an accident. In the meantime the family worries and wrings its hands and at last writes or goes to the nearest seamen's institute to ask it to find the wanderer. The institute has a way of combing the waterfront — not of America alone but of the whole world — for the lost one.[88]

From September 29 to December 31, 1919, 176 men were inquired for and ninety-three were found through Mother Roper's Missing Men Department. Thereafter, the number of missing men found each year became a statistic proudly cited in the Institute's Annual Report. At the time of Roper's death in 1943, the Department of Missing Men had helped to locate more than 6,500 mariners given up for lost.

Some years earlier, Mansfield had decided that seafarers needed decent medical care and that he would provide that, too. Sailors had access to the city dispensary, but foreign seamen, especially, were at a disadvantage in a strange port. At the Institute, staff translators were always available: the Reverend Vincent Tuzzio, who spoke Spanish; the Reverend Carl Ljunggren, Swedish; the Reverend Maximilian Pinert, German; Pastor Rasmus Andersen, Danish; and the Reverend Carl Podin, "the Chaplain of Many Tongues." So, in the fateful summer of 1914 Twenty-five opened a medical clinic, setting up operations with an examination table, an instrument cabinet, a sterilizer, a small assortment of simple surgical instruments, and a rudimentary stock of medicines, drugs, ointments, and bandages. At first the two visiting doctors (who donated their services) worked without even a blood-pressure cuff or microscope, making do with what they had and treating 800 patients during the first year. By 1920, the clinic had its own Dr. Wilson, who offered both acute and preventive care to an average of 750 seafarers monthly. One old salt, visiting the clinic, described it this way: "I am going into dry dock to have my hull examined and possibly have some repairs made to my machinery. I have plenty of boiler capacity, but somehow I can't keep up steam."[89] Like the Post Office, however, the clinic became too much to manage, and Mansfield had to solicit outside help. By the late 1920s, the medical clinic at the Institute was supervised by the United States Public Health Service.

Mansfield's humane concern for seafarers' health extended far beyond their shoreside well-being, and in 1920 he began to focus on the dismal state of medicine on merchant vessels at sea. By then there was a law on the books requiring all vessels to carry medicine chests, but, as Mansfield astutely pointed out to the annual meeting of the board of supervising inspectors of the Steamboat Inspection Service, what is the good of a medicine chest if no one is trained to use it, or if it doesn't reliably contain what it should? The answer was simple, Mansfield told the inspectors. Every candidate for the license of second officer or third engineer should be required to present evidence that he has completed a course in instruction in the principles of first aid. Such a course could easily be designed by the U.S. Public Health Service for this particular purpose, and the Public Health Service could also certify that each candidate had passed the course.[90]

Meanwhile, seafarers continued to die at sea because of the lack of training of their officers and the hit-or-miss contents of nonstandardized medicine chests. "If we had known what to do we could have saved his life!" a sailor wailed poignantly over the coffin of a friend being buried from the Institute's chapel one morning. The Institute's Captain Robert Huntington, already working on the problem of standardizing seagoing medicine chests, had an idea: Since the use of radios had become prevalent at sea, why not use the wireless to send "healing messages" to vessels at sea?

Later, he was modest about his role in promoting this lifesaving practice. "Well, perhaps you might say I thought of it," he admitted in an interview in the early 1920s. "But it was really nothing to my credit. I'd been at sea and run up against the lack of doctors' help hundreds of times. I'd seen fine sailors die and be buried at sea just because of that lack, when a little expert advice might have saved their lives — why, I'd have been a dumbbell if I hadn't thought of it."[91] Henry A. Laughlin of Philadelphia gave substance to Huntington's vision: He provided Huntington with $5,000 to install a long-range antenna and radio shack alongside the flying bridge and other roof structures at 25 South Street. Huntington applied for and obtained a limited commercial radio license, and on November 18, 1920, Radio KDKF came into being.

Almost immediately, Dr. Wilson, with Huntington's help, was busy taking medical histories via radio and "sending health through the air." Before long, whenever there was a medical problem on board ship, the captain would say, "Send me Sparks" (all ships' wireless men were called "Sparks"), and Sparks would radio Wilson, soon known to thousands of seafarers as "the mysterious Dr. KDKF."[92]

As happened with many of Mansfield's schemes, KDKF quickly became so successful as to be unmanageable by the Institute's hard-pressed staff, and outside help was called in. First, the Marine Hospital at Hudson and Jay Streets offered to furnish free medical advice during the hours Wilson and other Institute doctors were unavailable, any time of day or night, to be sent by radio to vessels under all flags. Then, in April 1921, the Institute's commercial radio

KDKF. An SCI doctor uses the wireless to send "healing messages" to vessels at sea in the early 1920s.

license was extended to the full twenty-four hours, and on May 12 a continuous watch was established by experienced radio operators in the Institute's radio station, in communication with the Marine Hospital by a special telephone line installed for that purpose.

Still, Mansfield wasn't satisfied. The range of the equipment on the roof of 25 South Street was limited to a radius of 1,200 miles under normal conditions, so in November 1921, Mansfield called David Sarnoff at the Radio Corporation of America and asked if RCA would take over KDKF. Sarnoff came down to see Mansfield, and within a few days RCA began to make arrangements to set up other stations in Chatham, Massachusetts; Siasconet, Massachusetts; Bush Terminal Building, Brooklyn; Cape May, New Jersey; and San Francisco. Hospitals in Key West, New Orleans, and San Francisco, among others, agreed to furnish medical advice to nearby stations.

Meanwhile, early in 1921, Mansfield, with the support of Assistant Surgeon General C.H. Lavinder, had convinced the inspectors of the Steamboat Inspection Service to agree to his proposal regarding first-aid training for prospective officers and engineers. "On and after December 31, 1921," the inspectors ruled, "no candidate for original license as master, mate, pilot, or engineer shall be examined until he shall present satisfactory evidence to the inspectors that he has completed a course in the principles of first-aid approved by the U.S. Public Health Service...."[93] That accomplished, Mansfield produced a simple, intelligent *First Aid Manual*, which was published jointly by the Institute and the Public Health Service in October 1921. His other iron in the fire, the standardization of medicine chests aboard ship, awaited action in the Department of Commerce."[94]

In its wide-ranging concern for the seafarer's welfare, the Institute took responsibility not only for a sailor's health but also for his professional competence. In 1914, in addition to the medical clinic, the Institute had opened a school of navigation. Commodore Arthur Curtiss James of the New York Yacht

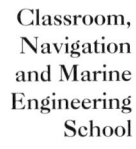

Classroom, Navigation and Marine Engineering School

Captain Robert Huntington with a student

Club and others had recently purchased and presented to the West Side YMCA the nearly defunct New York Nautical College on West 57th Street, established in 1882 for the purpose of helping seamen to become officers. The YMCA, which wanted to open the school downtown, approached the Institute in hopes of collaboration, and the school was moved to 25 South Street.[95]

The school was soon crowded with an odd assortment of yachtsmen, old salts, and fresh-faced kids who had been to sea as cabin boys and wanted to move up in the world. But by February 1916, it had become apparent that the cooperative plan between SCI and the YMCA would not succeed, as the two institutions were located too far apart to work together effectively. The YMCA generously decided to withdraw from the project, leaving all its materials and equipment at the disposal of the Institute. Steps were taken at once toward reorganization, and in June of that year, the name was changed to the Navigation and Marine Engineering School of the Seamen's Church Institute of New York.

Captain Robert Huntington, who later would pioneer the "health through the air" radio program, was appointed to oversee it. A Texan by birth, Huntington was a retired ship captain who had run a navigation school in Boston. He was described by one of his contemporaries as "a typical 'Cap'n,' bluff and hearty, with a resounding laugh and the twinkliest gray eyes in the world."[96] Huntington undertook advertising a bit more aggressively than his predecessor. "Prepare!— TO BE an OFFICER" newly printed flyers proclaimed, inviting applications from any seaman nineteen years old and a citizen, with three years' experience on any sail or steam vessel of 300 gross tons.

Of 306 students enrolled at the Institute school during 1917, some twenty-four received commissions in the United States Navy. By then, of course, the United States was at war. Courses in gunnery, ordnance, and signaling were added to the school's curriculum, taught by volunteer instructors, as well as preparatory classes for admission to Annapolis. The little steamship *J. Hooker Hamersley* was drafted as a part-time training vessel. In February 1918, the Engineering Department of the school was organized; students who successfully completed this program earned licenses as chief and second or third engineers. That summer, the school's new ship's bridge was completed on the roof of 25 South Street, inspiring Spaeth to rhapsodize, "You have a thrilling sense of being on the hurricane deck when you stand beside the flag-mast, holding onto the rail and looking across the sun-flecked bay and out through the Narrows. . . . It [seems] incredible that the 'ship' has not moved out of port, picking her graceful course between Governors Island and Liberty."[97] With the addition of a pilothouse and chart room, the school had everything it needed to turn out the licensed officers in demand to man the great number of vessels necessary to carry supplies to Allied troops fighting in France.

That was during the war. In its aftermath, the Institute perforce found itself less concerned with advancing sailors to higher rank than to getting them to sea at all. Suddenly, in the early 1920s, the bottom fell out of shipping. The December 1920 *Lookout* reported that hundreds of men were out of employment and could not get work of any kind. Shipping was "dull, very dull." By February of 1921, it was worse. The Shipping Board and other firms tied up hundreds of vessels, and thousands of sailors walked the streets looking in vain for work. In March, there were 20,000 seamen unemployed and 500 ships with sailings indefinite. In the fall of that year, at the same time Mansfield was making phone calls to David Sarnoff at RCA and publishing his *First Aid Manual*, he was also

---

THE CHAPLAIN'S OFFICE, 1920

"This is a great place, this office," a chaplain said one day in 1920 as he leaned back in his chair and watched two seamen walking toward the stairs, "here we see the world pass, and we give it a helping hand."

The following from the Chaplain's Office Log Book for August 19, 1920, illustrates a typical morning's work at the Institute in those days:

R. Macdonald to see doctor. Dressed superficial scald on shoulder.

Prepared affidavit certificates for seamen in lieu of identification [papers].

Richard Hill complaining of assault by Chief Engineer on high seas wants to have the man arrested. Advised to see [the Seamen's Branch of] the Legal Aid Society, 1 Broadway.

Sent three men to House Clinic.

Prepared three sets of affidavits of birth for seamen to use as identification when signing on.

Edward F. Sawyer advised that army discharge is sufficient.

John Toot advised about alien passport.

Unfair wage question discussed with tug man.

Seaman wishes ticket for west coast.

Michael Pilger — letter written for passport.

Leo Hubert — cash loan $2.

Institute passport made out for J. H. Hetur, a Swede.

British seaman asks for relief — referred to British and Canadian Patriotic Fund.

Roumanian wishes to aid parents, is directed how to send help.

Three Spanish firemen in search of work are directed to our Shipping Office.

Man directed how to get citizens' papers.

Officers directed to Officers' Unions.

Irishman cannot get passport — directed him to Custom's House.

— from *The Lookout*, September 1920

busy supervising work at the 39th Street Ferry House to convert it into a temporary relief station for destitute merchant seamen.

Men's shelter at Ferry House

Even the normally upbeat Institute staffers began to feel the strain. There were so *many* sailors out of work. "I do not know how I can talk to these men tonight," groaned one of the chaplains as he went off to conduct the Tuesday gospel service one evening. "How can I expect them to listen to me when I know they are hungry and some of them almost desperate?"[98]

At the Ferry House, about a block away from the Institute, Mansfield raced to finish the temporary relief headquarters before the cold weather set in. Out-of-work seafarers were sleeping in parks and doorways, any place they could find shelter from the wind. The relief headquarters was a result of a huge cooperative effort by the mayor's committee on relief and more than a dozen other agencies. The tireless Mansfield, serving on the mayor's committee on relief and the sub-committee on housing and feeding homeless men, was in charge of readying the Ferry House to receive the 500 men a night they hoped to shelter. Besides providing beds, hot showers, laundry facilities, and lunch, Mansfield wanted to move Twenty-five's Employment Bureau to the Ferry House for an all-out effort to secure work for the men. Only unemployed merchant seamen were to be given shelter, and they would have to give proof of their right to be taken in.

The relief headquarters was ready in time, and during the winter of 1921-22, 500 men a night were sheltered. But the unemployment situation worsened. Even with the relief headquarters, there was not enough room, and in 1922 approximately 27,000 seafarers were refused lodgings because there was no place to put them.[99]

Indeed, by 1923 there was some question whether the United States would continue to have a merchant marine at all. The U.S. government had on its hands a fleet of 1,500 steamships, most built during the war effort, which the private sector, despite prodding and pleading, refused to buy. A ship subsidy bill, which would encourage the private sector to buy some of these ships, had stalled in Congress, and in the following years the perennial question was endlessly debated: Should we have a strong merchant marine or not? Many felt America had been caught with its pants down during the recent war: Europe had clamored for American goods, America had produced those goods, and they had languished and rotted in railway cars backed up from the docks for miles because there were not enough ships to carry the goods to Europe. Yet no one wanted to pay the cost of keeping the merchant marine healthy in peacetime.

As the arguments for and against subsidization droned on, out-of-work mariners desperately turned to shoreside occupations. *The Lookout* pleaded with readers to consider hiring seafarers as handymen, or even as housekeepers: "Many of our men are splendid cleaners and they can paint and keep a place ship-shape as they call it; many others are cooks and stewards."[100] A number of sailors on the beach found work as building superintendents. As the *New York Times* pointed out, "Landlords and building management experts became aware of the desirability of ship-trained men as skipper and crew for their property." The sailors-turned-supers were far better prepared to deal with routine emergencies than previous incumbents, particularly the seafaring engineers. "Maintaining eight pounds of steam in his oil-burning heating plant," the *Times* explained, "is no hardship for a man who has kept up eighty to one hundred pounds of pressure on transports that ploughed nervously over the Atlantic during the war."

The postwar depression in shipping brought home to Mansfield, Baylies, and the board of managers the fact that the work of the Seamen's Church Institute had grown beyond the capacity of its physical plant. Every morning when Mansfield came to work, he passed men lined up from the hotel desk to the front door, waiting for 10 A.M. when the rooms would be put on sale. The number of beds was increased from 518 to 714 by converting the game room on the third floor into a dormitory, but still the line snaked out the door.

So, despite the poor economic climate, SCI made plans to expand. In 1924, the board of managers announced a new building fund to raise $1,900,000 for an annex to the present building. On January 26, 1925, a demolition crew began to tear down the old buildings on Front Street from Coenties Slip to Cuyler's Alley, including the saloon on the corner of Front Street and Coenties Slip that for fifty years had "fattened on the weaknesses of seamen,"[101] and on November 5, 1925, the cornerstone of the Annex was laid, with a dedication speech by Rear Admiral William S. Sims and an invocation by Bishop William T. Manning. The grand total required to pay for the land and the building was now estimated at $2,750,000.

During the summer of 1926, the shell was completed but interior construction was halted due to lack of funds; the board of managers scrambled to raise

MANSFIELD'S DREAM HOTEL

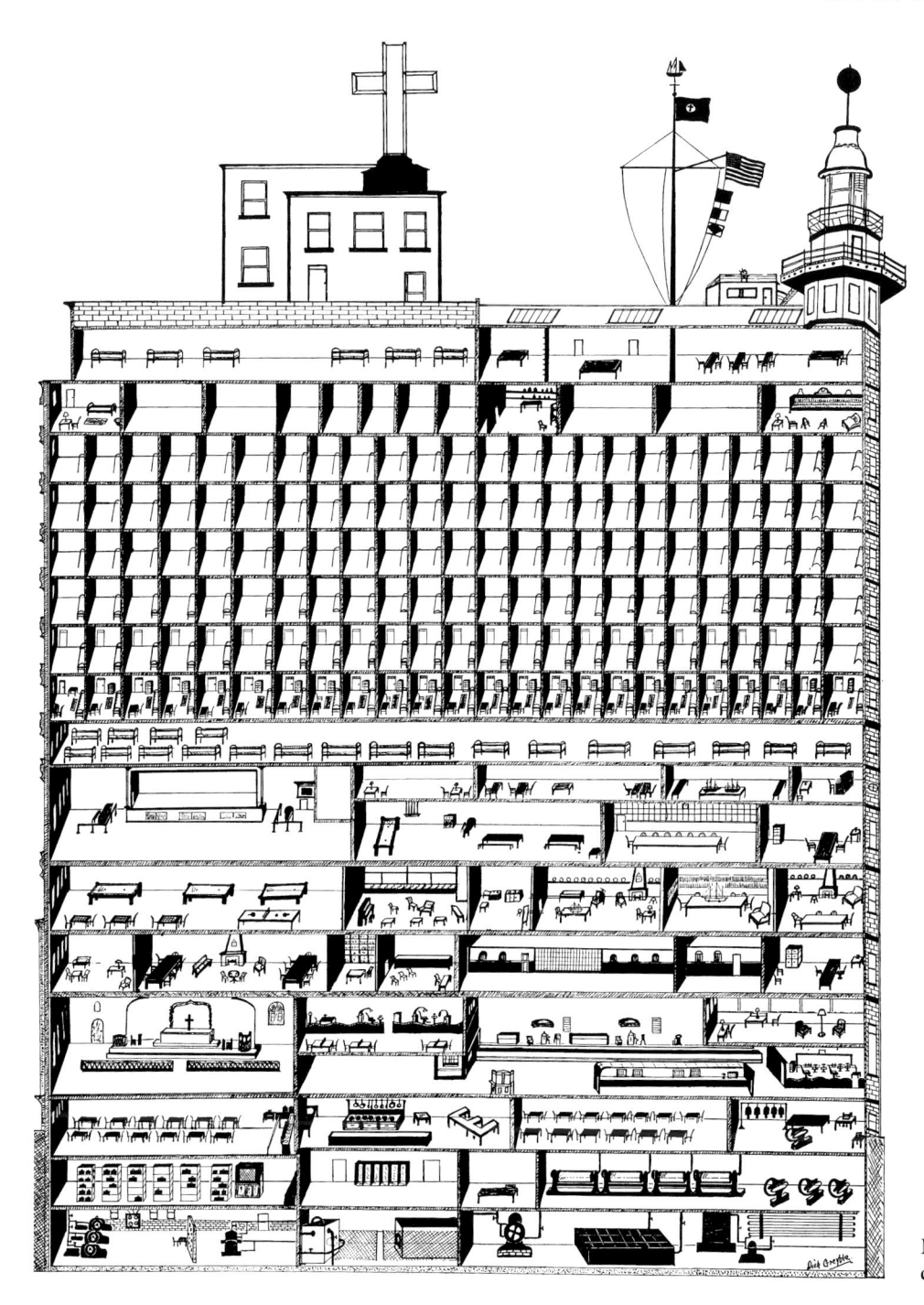

Mansfield's dream hotel during World War I

the $1,500,000 it needed to proceed. Thereafter, work sputtered along according to the vagaries of the economy and donors' pocketbooks. In 1927, John D. Rockefeller, Jr., donated $250,000, and the New York diocese pledged $50,000 to construct the new chapel. Even so, the board had to borrow $525,000 in short-term notes so that the building could be furnished and put into operation.

After a brief rally in shipping conditions in 1926, the economy seesawed down again. The winter of 1928, despite the mild weather, was the hardest winter in terms of unemployment since 1921. Coal strikes in Pennsylvania and the closing of textile mills in New England flooded New York City with jobseekers. Some of these men became "trip-ers" — they went to sea for a trip or two, competing with career seafarers for the dwindling number of jobs. Trip-ers also got hold of discharges, which entitled them to consideration at 25 South Street, where they competed for beds and relief funds and swelled the ranks of those besieging the Institute's Employment Bureau for berths aboard outgoing vessels. By March 1928, the Relief Department at Twenty-five had spent two-thirds of its funds for the calendar year. During 1928, the Institute's Employment Bureau was able to place only 5,040 seafarers, compared to the 6,325 it had placed in 1927. (Despite this gloomy economic situation, SCI staffers managed to stage a joyous dedication of the new Edmund Lincoln Baylies lobby in the recently completed Institute Annex.)

The economy seesawed again, and in 1929 there was a brief rally in employment — the Employment Bureau placed 8,637 seafarers in jobs, although 1,755 of the jobs were on land — but just as things were looking up, calamity struck in the form of the stock-market crash of 1929. The bottom fell out of all job markets. The Annual Report for 1930 noted that "our employment work has fallen off by *fifty percent*" — only 4,467 jobs were procured through the Employment Bureau that year. Out-of-work seamen from Boston, Baltimore, Philadelphia, and other nearby ports crowded into New York and found no work there, either. SCI staffers watched, amazed and dismayed, as the longest line of destitute, unemployed seafarers anyone could remember — with the exception of the winter of 1921 — spilled out the Institute's doors and snaked down the street.

During normal times, from thirty to forty unemployed mariners might apply for relief to the Institute's Religious and Social Work Department in a given month; in October 1930, seventy-five to eighty seafarers made application every day. Each afternoon, the men waited for meal and bed tickets. Trained ship's officers, who usually had no trouble shipping out, now stood in line with ordinary seamen. Self-respecting able-bodied seamen who had never accepted relief were compelled to seek the Institute's relief hospitality. Continually hammering home the ideal of "self-respect" (the modern social-work term might be *empowerment*), the Institute made a point of dispensing "loans" whenever feasible instead of out-and-out charity, which SCI staffers considered demoralizing and humiliating. Instead of a bread line, the Institute operated a "relief-loan" line and offered qualified seafarers credit in the form of lodging and food. A special "relief-loan" dormitory was "temporarily" set up with 100 army cots and adequate washing facilities.

Curiously, at the same time the longest line of relief-seekers was stretching out the door, the longest line of depositors at the Institute's "bank" in anyone's memory was also waiting. Because of the shipping crisis, seamen who had berths were not signing off at the end of each trip as they usually did. They were sticking steadily to work, taking their wages to the bank or sending money home, then sailing out again on the same ships. With such a small turnover, their unemployed brethren discovered that it was well nigh impossible to find vacancies with the majority of shipping companies. In the stewards' depart-

Shooting the sun on the Institute's roof during the 1920s

ments of passenger liners, fewer men were employed because the percentage of first-cabin travelers to Europe had dropped. Also, the advent of oil-burning motors and other modern equipment aboard ship reduced the crews needed. So again in 1931, the Institute's Employment Bureau found fifty percent fewer jobs: 2,306 jobs was the yearly total, down from the 4,467 of the year before. The number halved yet again in 1932, the blackest year, when only 1,455 jobs were found — and that figure included 650 jobs on land, most of them temporary.

According to the *New York Times*, in January 1931 the Seamen's Church Institute was visited *daily* by 8,000 to 12,000 merchant seamen. At the same time, it was estimated that 20,000 seafarers arrived in the Port of New York every day. If these same seafarers stayed an average of three days in port, leaving only when they shipped again, 50,000 to 60,000 of them thronged the city at any given time. But in 1931, only two or three percent of the seafarers clamoring for work actually got work.[102] The rest were "on the beach." Many of them were foreigners, not eligible to receive sustained help from public funds. Even American citizens who were not bona-fide residents of New York City were seldom entitled to relief from public and private welfare agencies. Hospitals and churches all over the metropolitan area, who did not consider seafarers their responsibility, referred them to 25 South Street. Thus, seafarers fell into a no-man's land

1927 cross on roof. On April 15, 1927, fifteen years after the *Titanic* went down, an illuminated cross on the roof of 25 South Street was dedicated as a tribute to the men of the merchant marine. President Coolidge in Washington pressed a button at 9 P.M., sending an electric current that illuminated the cross for the first time. Twenty feet high and twelve feet across, the cross rose forty-six feet above the roof and gave off a glow visible to ships turning in from the sea past Sandy Hook.

SEAMEN'S CHURCH INSTITUTE

During the Depression, the line of destitute seafarers often snaked around the block.

"between the devil of despond and the deep blue sea," as one reporter of the time put it.

For those who did not make their way through the doors of the Seamen's Church Institute, or who arrived there to find no room at the inn — the Institute's relief budget and income from endowment were only sufficient to meet the needs of about one-third of those seeking aid, and the lodging capacity was only 1,600 — the outlook was bleak. As they had during hard times in the winter of 1921-22, sailors took any jobs they could get. "Hundreds of deep-water sailors, caught 'on the beach' in New York by a puzzling landlubber mishap called the depression, find themselves driven to much ingenuity in finding work these days," the *Post* reported.[103] They worked as steeplejacks, window washers, Wall Street messengers, painters of anything from canoes and porch railings to flagpoles and barbers' mirrors, polishers of brass eagles and gilt ornaments in theaters — anything to tide them over the hard times. As the situation worsened, SCI in July 1931 instituted a special ten-cent dinner, served daily between three and four P.M., and 300 to 400 unemployed seafarers lined up each day — 500 a day, after word spread. In October, the ten-cent breakfast was established, which soon drew an average daily attendance of 250 at the soda fountain and 425 in the cafeteria. Many of the seafarers who ate these meals did so on the Institute's relief-loan system. During 1931, 7,998 merchant seamen were given relief through the Institute's Relief-Loan Department.

In October 1932, as philanthropists searched for new solutions, Harry Acton, shipping news reporter for the *New York American*, was covering the midnight sailing of the *Majestic* when he had the idea of charging a dime to visit these big liners and see the great leaders in industry, the arts, and sports — all the gossip-column swells — go aboard, en route to Europe. Through Acton's tireless efforts and the sympathetic cooperation of the Transatlantic Passenger Conference and the American Steamship Owners Association, the idea became a reality. Half of the money collected went to the Joint Emergency Committee, which daily fed and lodged 1,000 destitute seafarers in the Port of New York; the other half was given to seamen's welfare organizations in the home ports of the ships. Between October 1932 and March 1933, $7,927 was collected for the joint committee by this method. Still, it was just a drop in the bucket. As one historian noted, "A fog of despair hung over the land."[104] One out of every four American workers lacked a job. Franklin Delano Roosevelt, at his inauguration on March 3, 1933, put his hand on the family Bible open to the thirteenth chapter of I Corinthians, "For now we see through a glass darkly."

Some saw more darkly than others. The Depression was a fertile time for radical groups and activist protesters of all kinds, and as conditions worsened, the Institute found itself caught up in the Communist drive against "capitalistically owned property" and the war of Communists against conservative labor. Membership in the International Seafarers' Union fell off precipitously as the Marine Transport Workers branch of the Industrial Workers of the World — the "Wobblies," as they were called — usurped the place among seamen formerly held by the ISU. The Marine Transport Workers Union blasted the Institute, claiming it was part of an insidious program financed by the shipowners to subvert the sailor with good works.[105] The Waterfront Unemployed Council (an arm of another group with socialist leanings, the Marine Workers Industrial Union) published a malicious newsletter lampooning SCI, called "The Dog House News"; the "Dog House" was what the radicals called 25 South Street. Other snide monikers in this publication were "the Seamen's Prostitute," "the Destitute," and "the Holy Racket"; Mansfield became "the Holy Goat" and Roper was "the Madame."

The radicals did not shun violence. In November 1931, the police foiled a plot for the wholesale bombing of barges in New York Harbor; they arrested five members of the Independent Tidewater Boatmen's Union, all of whom gave

Seafarers gathered daily in the cafeteria in 1931.

Burial service. SCI chaplains officiated at burial and committal services so that seafarers without relatives would not be consigned to Potter's Field. When a seaman died, the Institute arranged for an undertaker, organ music, flowers for the altar, and burial in the Institute's plot at Cedar Grove Cemetery or at Evergreen Cemetery.

the Institute as their address.[106] In July 1932, Communists staged a protest on the main floor at 25 South Street and tried to rush the Social Services Department, but they were stopped by the Institute's special police officers, who turned the ringleader over to the New York Police Department. Several weeks later, twenty-five unemployed members of MWIU stormed the doors. Shouting imprecations against hotel manager Leslie C. Westerman, they demanded, among other things, free meals for all unemployed; free access to dunnage at all times (SCI's Baggage Department charged a small fee for checking or retrieving dunnage); additional free beds; and free use of bathing facilities. Due to a summer rainstorm, the Institute was crowded with more than two thousand sailors; about fifty of them went to the aid of the three special police officers. In the melee that followed, several shots were fired, amazingly striking no one. The battle raged for an hour, sweeping through Twenty-five's public rooms with a wreckage of furniture before spilling out onto the street, where a dozen brawls ranged along the East River.[107]

In November 1932, when Communist agitators threatened to disrupt SCI's annual benefit theater night, NYPD mobilized fifty patrolmen and twenty plainclothes detectives to guard the Henry Miller Theater, stationing a uniformed officer every twenty feet along 43rd Street from Broadway to Sixth Avenue. The MWIU demonstrators, demoralized, stood down.

There were some bright spots during these troubled times. Mansfield, who frequently emphasized that the relief work so much in the foreground now was only part of the Institute's program for sailors, opened the William D. Tracy Dental Clinic and the John Markle Eye Clinic in the fall of 1931. Mansfield's dream was to complete an Institute health center comprising various units — medical, dental, eye, orthopedic, and genito-urinary. In 1932, the Institute opened a barbershop where thirty-five men a day got free haircuts, and a free shoe-repair shop where seafarers who had been pounding the pavement looking for work could obtain new leather soles and thick rubber heels. Vincent Caracoglia, the cobbler, set up his shoe-repair shop in the Institute's basement. He could re-sole fifteen pairs of shoes a day. "The top part of a lot of the shoes are pretty badly worn," he noted, "but I manage to fix them up. The men all ask for heavy soles so they won't wear out so fast while they hunt for work."[108] Through the generosity of loyal Institute donors who contributed to the Holiday Fund each year, the Institute was able to provide bountiful Thanksgiving and Christmas dinners. In 1930 the Institute arranged to serve Thanksgiving dinner to 1,500 seafarers for twenty-five cents each — free to those who were penniless — with a pack of cigarettes thrown in. That evening, a thousand seafarers packed the auditorium and watched the "all-talkie picture" *The Rogue Song*. In 1931, on Christmas Eve, each of the 1,354 seamen lodging in the building received a cheery red card wishing him "Merry Christmas" and entitling him to a free dinner — turkey, dressing, vegetables, cranberry sauce, mince pie, pumpkin pie, coffee, cigarettes, and cigars. In 1932, more than 1,400 seafarers were guests of the Institute for Christmas turkey dinner, and more than 1,300 comfort bags containing candy, fruit, sweaters, and stationery were distributed to sick and convalescent sailors at the U.S. Marine Hospitals at Stapleton, Staten Island, and on Ellis Island.

By New Year's Day 1934, there was some indication that the tide might be turning. "Shipping is beginning to improve," Mansfield noted cautiously in the February *Lookout*. "My hope for 1934 is to see our debt to the banks [for the Annex] removed so that we may continue a full program of service to the seafarers in this Port." Warily hopeful, SCI staffers and seafarers alike diverted themselves from their troubles to celebrate Mansfield's sixty-third birthday and thirty-eight years on the job at the Seamen's Church Institute.

On Sunday, February 11, 1934, Mansfield suffered a heart attack and died at his apartment at 40 Fifth Avenue. "With characteristic vigor," Marjorie Dent Candee, editor of *The Lookout*, later reported, "Dr. Mansfield was working on Institute matters up to the very last."

Stunned, more than two thousand sailors attended Mansfield's funeral, many of them standing silently on the sidewalk outside the Institute, others mingling with the executives of important steamship lines and socially prominent women who packed the pews and aisles of the Chapel of Our Saviour. While the ship's bell of the old *Atlantic* tolled a one-minute-interval knell, Bishop Manning intoned the prayer of rest for the dead. Flags throughout the port hung at half-mast. Mansfield "not only preached and prayed for the sailor," eulogized the *New York Times*, "but fought for him against mercenary and vicious forces that once made this 'the worst seaport for seamen in the world.' He left it the best."[109]

"The time may come when we will be accustomed to enter a room without his cheery greeting and to conduct our meetings without his presence," Herbert L. Satterlee said afterward, speaking on behalf of the board, "but it is not yet."[110]

Mother Roper

On April 6, 1943, word went out along the waterfront that Mother Roper had passed on.

The seafaring world was dismayed. Hardly a seafarer had not heard of her. She was "Battling Roper, the South Street Champ," who was unafraid to enter the saloons of Sailortown to find a man she wanted to talk to. She was "Mother of 50,000 Sailors," because she felt a sailor could always use a home-away-from-home and a Mom away-from-Mom. She was "The Lady Who Listens." President Franklin D. Roosevelt, hearing of her death, wrote one of her daughters, "Men of the sea from all over the world brought their problems to her in full confidence of sympathetic understanding and practical helpfulness."

Most important of all, she was "Mrs. Roper, who locates Wandering Boys." The woman who mailed the *Missing Seamen Bulletin* to ports around the world. The woman who went on the radio to take her inquiries to an even larger audience. In January 1934, Mother Roper traveled to Washington, DC to join Captain Phillips Lord's radio program aboard the four-masted ship *Seth Parker*, at that time anchored in the Potomac River. Hundreds of radio listeners heard her soft, clear voice:

> Boys who are sailing out on the sea and listening in tonight: Find for me — Smoky Joe — His mother is dying. Tell Harry Kelly — Punch Kelly — his father has died and his mother has got to go to the poorhouse. . . . Shorty McGuire has been looking for his wife and little boy. Tell him I've finally located [them] — and they want him back. Goodnight, Boys — and see that you write your Mother and your sweetheart once a month and let them know where you are. That's only fair play. Goodnight, boys.[111]

Shortly thereafter, Roper said she was answering as many as thirty letters a day, from listeners who had heard her broadcasts and had written to implore her to find a long-lost son, brother, husband, father, or nephew. "I grieve for the lonely mothers who are counting on me to perform miracles and restore their lost sons," Roper said simply.[112]

She was born to it, Roper often explained. Her mother, Marion Lord, with little Janet in tow, used to canvas the Newfoundland ports, meeting ships, talking to seafarers, fruitlessly asking after her brother Jimmy who had gone to sea and had not been heard from since. Uncle Jimmy died in Calcutta and a letter came, from a woman who had nursed him during his final illness. The outings along the wharves, speaking with seamen, going from ship to ship, stopped. But still Janet sang the song she had learned at her mother's knee: "Uncle Jimmy is on a ship; Uncle Jimmy is coming back."

In her youth, Janet moved with her family to Boston, and one day, when she was about seventeen, she found herself mesmerized by a clergyman from the Boston Seamen's Friend Society, who had come to give a talk on seamen's missions at Janet's church. "What can I do to help?" she blurted out afterward. Thus began her ministry to those who go down to the sea in ships. She started out as a Bible teacher. But by the time she was nineteen, she was visiting deep-water boardinghouses, ships, and shipping offices.

Janet Lord married the Reverend Harry Roper, a young Andover graduate and former New Brunswick fisherman, on August 1, 1894. The newlyweds moved to Westford Village, Massachusetts, where Harry became rector of the local Episcopal Church.

When Harry's health failed, Janet took over his priestly duties, writing her own sermons, ascending into the pulpit to give them, and even officiating at funerals — in addition to caring for the couple's three young daughters and for Harry on his sickbed. Eventually tiring of what Harry called "pink tea" religion, the Ropers moved to St. John, New Brunswick, where Harry took the post of chaplain at the Seamen's Institute. It was during her time in St. John that she was first called "Mother Roper" by cadets on a training ship. They liked her for her "straight-from-the-shoulder talk,"[113] and she began to lean more and more toward the social-work aspects of her ministry. She discouraged drunkenness and vice not because they were sins but because they contributed to the deplorable social status of seamen as misfits and irresponsibles. Seek diversion away from waterfront influences, she counseled the men.

Despite his precarious health, Harry Roper was called to the Seamen's Institute in Portland, Oregon, where he and his wife took up his duties in 1906; again, Janet worked alongside her husband, and frequently in his place.

After nine years in Portland, Harry died of pneumonia in March 1915. By July of the same year, Janet had arrived at 25 South Street, invited by Mansfield to fill the recently created post of house mother. At first her work was general. Trouble of any kind at the Institute — trouble at the hotel desk, in the baggage room, anywhere — was taken to Mrs. Roper. "Mrs. Roper will fix it" became an axiom. Soon the seamen began taking their personal troubles to her to fix. She liked the role of "the listener," and she was good at it. Taciturn men became articulate in her presence. Younger men lost their shyness. She dispensed advice to the lovelorn and practical advice in other matters, too.

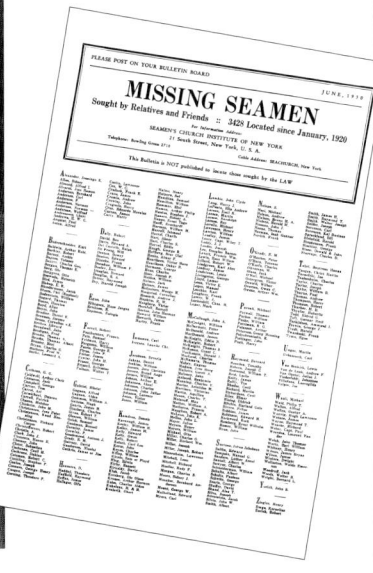

Finally, Roper tackled the job that would make her famous: locating missing seamen. During the First World War, she was deluged with inquiries about missing seamen. Soon her *Missing Seamen Bulletins* were being mailed to every important port in the world, where they were posted in sailors' homes and pubs, shipping agencies, and ship registration offices. Names were checked against ships' crews and identities were compared and reported to Roper. Many of the men were surprised to find they were "missing." As the Reverend James C. Healey, a former staff member at the Institute, once pointed out, "Seamen wander, seamen forget to leave their new addresses, and because fingers have fashioned themselves to the shape of a paint brush, marlinespike, or fire shovel, they bend with difficulty around the narrow limits of a pen."[114]

In 1931, the *New York World* reported that the "gray-haired, genial" Mrs. Roper "solves as many mysteries, picks up as many clews and gets as much evidence as a score of New York detectives."[115] During that year, Roper topped the 3,000 mark in missing men found. With the start of World War II, the volume of inquiries trebled, and Roper's fame had spread around the world. "Go to Mrs. Roper" was the advice seamen gave the families of missing men, and the families did. It might take months to get the information requested, but Roper never gave up.

Her funeral service was conducted in the Institute's Chapel of Our Saviour, on April 8, 1943, by SCI Director Dr. Harold H. Kelley and Chaplains McDonald and Harkness. "She has dropped her anchors in Snug Harbor," seafarer Arthur George Montagne wrote afterward, "but her Anchor Lights are so bright that sailors can see them around the world."[116]

75¢ ROOMS
RUNNING WATER
AND DAY OCCUPANCY

**ROOM AND
DORMITORY
ACCOMMODATIONS**

THE REMODELED AND
ENLARGED ROOMS ON THE
10TH FLOOR OLD BUILDING WILL
BE OPENED FOR INSPECTION
1 P.M. TO 2 P.M. DAILY

CHAPTER FIVE

The Second World War

At 11 A.M. on September 3, 1939, the British Royal Navy's worldwide network of wireless transmitters crackled with an electrifying signal to all His Majesty's ships: TOTAL GERMANY. The British government's two-hour ultimatum to Hitler's Reich to withdraw its troops from Poland had expired. Britain and France were at war with Germany.

An hour later, a second signal went out, over a different network to different listeners. OPEN HOSTILITIES WITH ENGLAND AT ONCE flashed to all ships of the Kriegsmarine, the German Navy. That afternoon, as Winston Churchill addressed Parliament and warned his fellow countrymen to expect "many disappointments, and many unpleasant surprises," Lieutenant Fritz-Julius Lemp, commander of the *U-30*, patrolling some 250 miles northwest of Ireland, eagerly readied his U-boat and crew to deliver the first of them. When informed just after 7:30 P.M. by his lookout on the conning tower that a ship had been sighted, Lemp, without a second look at what was obviously a passenger liner, submerged for the attack.

The SS *Athenia*, 13,581 tons, three days out of Glasgow, was bound for Montreal with 1,103 passengers and 305 crew. Most of the passengers, including many children and 300 Americans, were fleeing a war that had seemed imminent and was now real. They were about to become the first merchant marine casualties of it. A torpedo struck the *Athenia* squarely, a little aft of amidships, blowing away the stairs from the third-class and tourist dining saloons and cutting off escape from those areas to the upper decks. One hundred eighteen people, including twenty-eight Americans, died.

Of that fateful Sunday, Marjorie Dent Candee, editor of *The Lookout*, later wrote, "There flashed across the ocean two tragic messages: the one, that war drums again rolled in Europe, and the second, an SOS from the sinking liner *Athenia*." In the Port of New York, the shock of the war was felt at once, she

Room and dormitory accommodations. In February 1942, the Seamen's Church Institute became the official receiving station of the first American maritime "pool" ever established. After young men completed maritime service training, they were sent to the Institute to await calls to the merchant ships. SCI also quartered U.S. Signal Corpsmen who were making a special air-defense study of downtown New York, and members of the Coast Guard awaiting orders.

71

noted. "Carefully planned shipping schedules were thrown into the discard, marine insurance rates soared, thousands of travelers stranded abroad rushed for home. Great ocean liners, with portholes painted black, scurried into port, or steamed apprehensively out into the Atlantic."[117] At the Institute, a microcosm of the port, the shock of war seemed refracted through a magnifying glass. When passenger and cruise trips were canceled, SCI had to care for out-of-work seafarers. Numerous foreign crews were thrown out of work, their ships tied up for the duration and the seafarers quartered at 25 South Street until their consuls could ship them home. At the same time, New York suddenly became the supply depot for Great Britain, which imported all of its oil, most of its raw materials, and half of its food. Soaring wartime demands for these supplies translated into longer shore leaves for crews in New York while freighters were being loaded — and longer stays at the Institute.

Rescued crews of torpedoed vessels were brought to New York, and as their counterparts had done twenty-five years earlier, they went straight to the Institute. Captain Thomas Georgeson and his crew of thirty-six were among the first arrivals; their ship, the British freighter *Winkleigh*, was torpedoed by a German submarine on September 8, 1939. By mid-October, the Institute had lodged crews of the *Olivebank*, *Blairlogie*, *Heronspool*, and *Kafiristan*, among others, and SCI staffers and seafarers alike could concur with Churchill's description of the U-boat war: "hard, widespread and bitter, a war of groping and drowning, a war of ambuscade and stratagem, a war of science and seamanship."[118] In December 1939, Marjorie Dent Candee reported in *The Lookout* that 150 merchantmen, representing more than 600,000 tons, had gone down — by mine or torpedo — in the first twelve weeks of the war.

To all shipwrecked crews, SCI staffers dispensed shoes, socks, and underwear from the Institute's Sloppe Chest. Comfort bags containing shaving gear, toothbrushes, sewing kits, and other sundries were also provided. To one Javanese crew, strict Muslims who insisted on cooking their own food, SCI

SS *Athenia*. The first merchant marine casualty of World War II, the Anchor-Donaldson Line steamship *Athenia* was torpedoed by a German U-boat on September 3, 1939. One hundred eighteen people, including twenty-eight Americans, died.

U-Boat Victims Adrift in the Atlantic

Experiences of torpedoed crews led to advances in safety at sea, and by March of 1942, lifeboats were routinely stocked with such diverse supplies as massage oil (to help prevent frostbite in extremities stiff with cold); jackknives, can openers and bottle openers; concentrated foods (meat and vegetable tablets), and a new kind of biscuit that did not make people thirsty. Life preservers now came equipped with a red light that went on automatically when the wearer hit the water. Some more ad-hoc safety precautions also became commonplace. "Whenever a seaman threatens to drink salt water," one sailor explained, "an officer knocks him out."[119]

---

staffers after some initial bemusement obligingly provided spices, rice, and fish, allowing four of the Javanese full run of the Institute's galley to prepare it. Crews of British-owned vessels received the additional benefit of a new suit of clothing, paid for by the British Consulate through SCI's established arrangement with a department store.

In September 1940, the halls of the Institute suddenly echoed with the piping voices of 256 British child evacuees, ranging in age from four to fifteen. Under the auspices of the U.S. Committee for the Care of European Children, the children had been invited by the Institute's director, the Reverend Dr. Harold H. Kelley, to take temporary shelter at 25 South Street on their way to relatives or to American foster homes. Particularly delighted with the showers, the children presented a challenge to their volunteer attendants, who were hard pressed to keep some of them from taking two or three before breakfast. More conventional activities included visits to the aquarium, ice-cream parties in the Institute's Apprentice Room, and ping-pong and billiards with young British apprentices from the torpedoed crew of the Norwegian freighter *Tancred*. For the first time ever, a children's service was held in the Institute's chapel.

SEAMEN'S CHURCH INSTITUTE

Belgian crew. One of the last crews torpedoed in World War II, these seafarers pose for a photograph in front of 25 South Street.

Captain and crew of the torpedoed British freighter *Winkleigh* thank their rescuer, Captain G.J. Barendse of the *Statendam*.

After Holland was overrun by the Nazis in the spring of 1940, officials of the Netherland Shipping and Trading Committee approached Dr. Kelley and offered to finance a room for Dutch seafarers at the Institute. Dr. Kelley commandeered a large room on the third floor of the Institute, and Captain George Barendse, formerly of the Holland-America passenger liner *Statendam* — which rescued the crew from the *Winkleigh* and subsequently burned in the harbor of Rotterdam during the Nazi invasion — supervised the construction of the room, which was decorated with typically Dutch furnishings from Holland and from Heineken's Restaurant at the 1939 World's Fair. The "Home for Netherland Seamen" was opened officially on November 15, 1940, by the minister from the Netherlands, Dr. Alexander Loudon, who called on Dutch seamen to "be our front line which is at sea wherever ships move."

The Dutch home was so immediately popular that British and Belgian interests offered to finance similar club rooms at the Institute for their merchant seamen. On March 26, 1941, British Ambassador Lord Halifax visited the Institute to open the newly completed British Merchant Navy Club. On April 15, Camille Gutt, Minister of National Defense, Communications, and Finance of Belgium, opened the Belgian Seamen's Home, with rooms on the third floor alongside the Home for Netherland Seamen. Like the Dutch, the Belgians needed a place for sailors to feel at home for the duration; their country too had been overrun by the Nazis in the spring of 1940.

As in the First World War, SCI staffers considered recreation and entertainment indispensable to keeping up morale, and they scheduled movies; wrestling and boxing bouts; old-time vaudeville stunt nights or "smokers"; tournaments in pool, billiards, and bowling; and lectures and concerts in the Institute's auditorium. (In one ironic juxtaposition to the war, the 1939 New York World's Fair — allegedly promoting international cooperation — provided a diverting outing for torpedoed crews; the Institute arranged with fair authorities for free passes.) At the same time, the Institute, while heroic in its efforts to distract seafarers from the war, did not shrink from its responsibility to prepare them for it. In early 1940, the Institute opened a new signaling course in cooperation with the U.S. Navy so that merchant seamen and officers would be familiar with the Navy's signaling code, in the event of a "national emergency." The federal government, still officially isolationist in 1940 despite President Franklin Roosevelt's personal leanings, dared not breathe the word *war*.

The pages of *The Lookout* soon filled with heroic tales of merchant seafarers on Allied ships. Two seafarers, Wilbert Roy Widdicombe, twenty-four years old, and Robert George Tapscott, nineteen, survivors of the 5,956 ton freighter *Anglo-Saxon*, sunk in August 1940 by an armed raider, traveled 2,500 miles in an open boat, reaching Eleuthera in the Bahamas after seventy days at sea. Their lifeboat had been machine-gunned by the Germans and they had watched eight of their comrades die of exposure, gangrene, and starvation. Colonel Franklin Remington, a member of SCI's board of managers, was in Nassau when the two men came ashore, and he relayed the amazing tale to New York. "Listen to this epic of the sea," he wrote Marjorie Dent Candee. "It makes Captain Bligh's experience after leaving the *Bounty* seem like a jaunt on Long Island Sound."[120] This one particular war story, unlike most, ends on a light note. After weeks of hospitalization in the Bahamas, Widdicombe made his way to 25 South Street. Lionized by newspapers, magazines, radio programs, and various Caledonian societies, he approached the keeper of SCI's Sloppe Chest and confessed that he was desperately in need of a tuxedo to attend the Scotch Ball at the Waldorf-Astoria. The keeper magically produced a beautiful dinner jacket that fit Widdicombe so perfectly it might have been made for him.

The lighter moments were few and far between. In the "Battle of the Atlantic" — a phrase originally coined by Churchill to mean the struggle over the Anglo-American lifeline but that eventually encompassed a campaign of many sea battles spread over six years of war — merchant mariners were subjected to the indiscriminate warfare of magnetic mines, submarines, surface raiders, and air attacks. Men whose limbs had been blown away died of shock or gangrene

The Reverend Dr. Harold H. Kelley

Dr. Kelley succeeded the Reverend Dr. Archibald Mansfield as superintendent (as the director was then called) in 1934, after fifteen years of experience in seafarers' agencies in San Francisco and Los Angeles. Before that, after graduating from the University of California and the Church Divinity School of the Pacific, he was a missionary in Ketchikan, Alaska, and the rector of several churches on the west coast.

Kelley directed the Institute through the hard years of the Depression and the hectic time of war. Working at 25 South Street, he supervised the distribution of clothing and food to needy seafarers, oversaw the medical clinics, and solicited old eyeglasses and old shoes from the public through letters to the newspapers for the benefit of his charges.

In recognition of his aid to British, Danish, and Dutch crews during the Second World War, Kelley was appointed an officer of the Order of Orange-Nassau by Queen Wilhelmina of the Netherlands, and an honorary officer of the Order of the British Empire by King George VI. He also received the Danish King Christian X Medal of Liberations.

After fourteen years as director, Kelley retired, and in 1948 he returned with his wife to California. At his death on November 2, 1965, he was an associate at St. Mark's Episcopal Church in Berkeley.

---

in the open lifeboats; their companions often succumbed to exposure, thirst, or starvation when no one rescued them. Frequently no one *would* rescue them. An instructor at the U.S. Navy's Armed Guard branch at Little Creek, Virginia, had these grim instructions for men training in 1941 for duty aboard convoy escort ships:

> You will engage the enemy until your guns can no longer be fired. That means until the decks are awash and the guns are going under. Then you may abandon ship if you wish. But you must never expect another convoy ship to pick you up, nor may you permit your ship to stop for others. For the safety of the many, a ship in convoy must pass by all survivors in the sea. No stopping for anyone. Leave all rescues to the special rescue ships — if there are any.[121]

Luckily, some captains ignored these stipulations. But kindhearted captains frequently did not arrive on the scene quickly enough to do much good. A typical lifeboat saga was that of the fifty-two men who survived the torpedoing of the Belgian ship *Ville de Liege* on Easter Sunday 1941, only to find themselves adrift in open lifeboats in the chill and turbulent latitudes between Iceland and Greenland. The weather was stormy and the four lifeboats became separated. The captain's boat, with eleven men, capsized twice but was rescued after thirteen days. Five of the eleven men, including the captain, subsequently lost one or both legs to amputation due to gangrene. One man died. The other boats? One was found with three men, two living and one dead. A second was found bearing five dead men. The third was never found. Four of the amputee survivors of the *Ville de Liege* attended the 1941 Christmas Eve party at the British

Merchant Navy Club at the Institute and were given a rousing cheer by their fellow seafarers.[122]

For the most part, merchant mariners did their duty without fanfare, and anonymously. "No one turns in the street to admire their uniforms," an editor at the *New York Times* noted in 1942. "They wear no uniform. No one steps up to the bar to buy them drinks. No moist-eyed old ladies turn to them in the subway and murmur 'God bless you.'"[123] They did not advertise themselves, taking seriously the posters plastered on the walls of the Institute and elsewhere: "Loose Lips Sink Ships"; "Don't Tell Names of Ships, Destinations, or Cargoes"; "Don't Help the Enemy — Seamen Serve Silently." Many refused to talk to reporters. Some refused to talk even among themselves, maintaining a stoic silence. Others sought out the sympathetic SCI staffers in the Institute's Welfare Department and unburdened themselves. "The number of torpedoed seamen coming here seems to increase daily," one staffer wrote at the time, "and the terrific mental strain through which they go shows on many of them. Big, burly men whom you would never suspect of ever having shed a tear, break down and weep when they relate their experiences. But they vow to go out again."[124]

And go out again they did, despite the fact that for a long time, it looked as though Germany was winning the Battle of the Atlantic. During the first quarter of 1942, German U-boats sank 216 vessels in the North Atlantic — 1.25 million tons of shipping. In June of that year, the absolute worst month of the war for sinkings, 834,196 tons of Allied shipping was sunk worldwide, 700,000 of it in the North Atlantic.[125] The Germans referred to it as *die glückliche Zeit* (the "Happy Time"); Samuel Eliot Morison, the official U.S. historian, called it "a merry massacre."[126] Undaunted, the seafarers shipped out again and again. By the end of the year, some regulars at 25 South Street had been torpedoed four, five, even six times. In 1943, the tide finally turned — in August, the sinkings *of* U-boats surpassed the sinkings *by* U-boats — but in practical terms that meant only that fewer men died, not that men stopped dying altogether. The ones who weren't killed shipped out again.

When news of the Normandy invasion on June 6, 1944, flashed through the game rooms and lobbies of 25 South Street, most of the seafarers regretted deeply that they were not "over there" — even though many had just returned from carrying supplies that had made the invasion possible. "Seamen on well-deserved shore leaves flocked to War Shipping offices to sign on without delay," Marjorie Dent Candee marveled. "Their feeling duplicates that of seamen on freighters abroad who have been 'jumping ship' in England...so that they could sign on merchant vessels taking part in the initial landings in France."[127] Undaunted by the threat of air attacks, surface fire, U-boats, or coastal batteries, merchant seafarers carried their cargo across the English Channel to France and returned to Britain's shores to start a shuttle service that would not end until Germany's unconditional surrender.

V-E Day, when it arrived, was observed quietly and reverently at 25 South Street. Seafarers from Holland and Denmark, glued to the radios in their club rooms from the moment the first news broke, wept when the realization sank in

MERCHANT MARINE SCHOOL "FLYING BRIDGE" ATOP 25 SOUTH STREET

After Pearl Harbor, it became necessary for the Institute to literally "raise the roof" at 25 South Street to accommodate increased enrollment at the Merchant Marine School. The staff of instructors was enlarged to twenty-two. A 774-foot-long ship's pilothouse and flying bridge were added to the rooftop school. Dedicated as "The Pilot House, a memorial to Charles Hayden" (a member of the Institute's board of managers until his death in 1937), the structure was outfitted with all modern navigation devices, including a Sperry gyro and a "Metal Mike" for automatic steering and for taking bearings. The equipment was donated by the Sperry Company. In 1942, three hundred boys from thirty New York high schools got their first taste of navigation by enrolling at the Merchant Marine School as aeronautical cadets, under the supervision of the Institute's faculty. Instruction for these boys was free.

that they could go home. Many attended the emotional chapel service conducted by SCI's director Kelley and chaplain Harkness to give thanks for the cessation of hostilities in Europe. Then they shipped out again. The War Shipping Administration urged merchant seamen, officers, stevedores, and longshoremen to stick to their jobs—and they did. The doors of 25 South Street swung open all day long with seamen carrying duffel bags and suitcases, reporting to their ships.

On V-J Day, August 14, 1945, when the war was truly over, seafarers and staffers gathered on the flying bridge of the Merchant Marine School to take it all in. Pennants flew from all the ships in New York Harbor. Tankers, freighters, and tugs blasted their whistles in a thrilling cacophony of victory. Rocket flares shot up into the sky. Some seafarers made their way uptown to Times Square and other hot spots, where the main festivities seemed to be taking place. But many chose to celebrate at 25 South Street, at "home," with the SCI staffers who had looked after them during the long years of war.

The war had taken a terrible toll at sea. The Allies lost 2,828 of their own and neutral ships, or 14,687,231 gross-register tons, to submarines. The global total of merchant shipping lost was 5,150 vessels (21,570,720 tons). Of these, 2,452 (12.8 million tons) went down in the Atlantic.[128] According to the most authoritative tabulations available, 624 of the 6,000 American-flag vessels were sunk by enemy action, 130 were damaged, two were captured and used by the Japanese, 27 were deliberately scuttled to form artificial harbors off the Normandy beachheads, and 82 became marine casualties.[129]

How many people died in the campaign cannot be precisely computed. The British merchant navy lost 30,248 men.[130] Approximately 290,000 civilian seafarers served in the American Merchant Marine and Army Transportation Service at one time or another during hostilities. Of this number, 114,145 received the merchant marine combat ribbon. At least 6,103 Americans were killed while serving on merchant vessels. This averages to 9.8 fatalities per sinking, or approximately twenty percent of a typical crew of fifty. A further 1,760 men were wounded, and 609 were taken prisoner, fifty-four of these dying in Japanese prisoner-of-war camps. The American Merchant Marine and Army Transportation Service suffered 2.8 percent fatal casualties, the highest total of any branch of service except the Marine Corps.[131]

Yet a merchant seaman who had heard the victory news on the radio in the Janet Roper Room expressed the sentiment of many when he said, "After the first wonderful feeling that the war is over, I'm starting to realize what a lot of work there is ahead of us in getting our soldiers back home and in sending food and supplies to occupied and liberated countries."[132]

The very next day, the seafarers shipped out again.

The Duke and Duchess of Windsor greet seafarers at SCI's British Merchant Navy Club. During the war, it was not unusual to see well-known faces among visitors to the Institute. In addition to the Windsors, Crown Princess Juliana of the Netherlands was a celebrated guest.

V-E Day. Seafarers raise a toast in SCI's Belgian Seamen's Home.

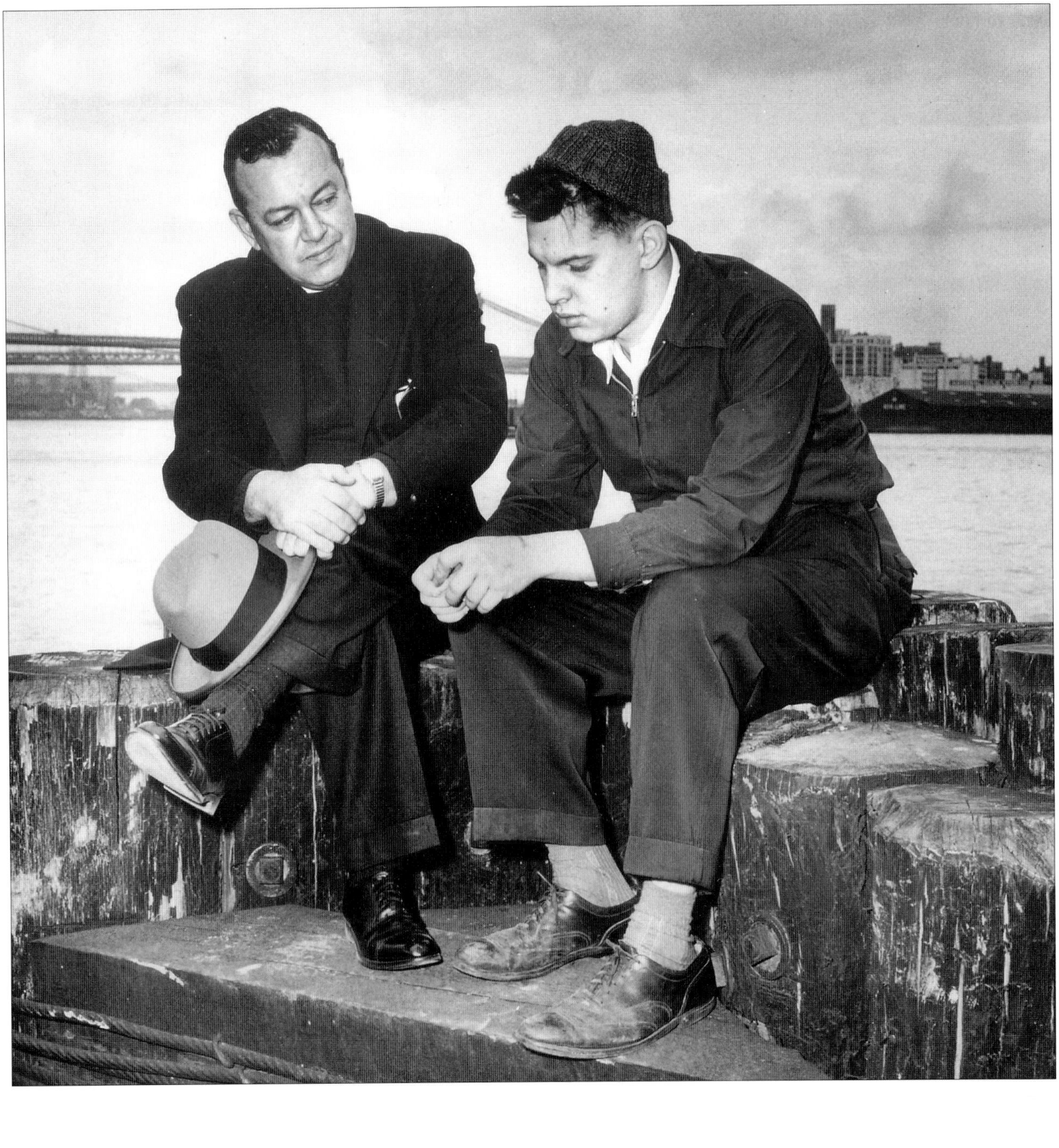

CHAPTER SIX

Sink or Swim

In January 1955, the black flag of piracy flew over Newport News, Virginia.

The coal ship *Seacoral*, like many American ships of her time, had been sold to foreign interests. The crew had hauled down the Stars and Stripes for the last time. In its place, they hoisted the skull and crossbones to protest their replacement by a crew of Greek seafarers when the vessel was put under Liberian registry. For six days the Jolly Roger flapped in the breeze while the *Seacoral*, having surrendered one registry and awaiting another, was officially a ship without a country.

In the 1950s, there were many who thought that the Jolly Roger might as well fly over the entire American merchant marine. In the absence of tariffs, which protected other industries, an increasing number of unsubsidized American ship operators were — with government sanction — transferring vessels to foreign flags in order to match the lower labor costs of their overseas competitors. They fired the American crews, hoisted the Liberian or some other flag, and then hired foreign seafarers, who were cheaper and less demanding than their American counterparts.

National Maritime Union statistics show that in the two-week period ending August 5, 1954, 19,625 American seafarers registered to ship but only 2,157 got berths. Overall figures for the industry indicate that in 1954, one job in every three that had existed in 1952 was no longer open to American merchant seamen.

Sadly, Americans didn't seem to care much. "Despite the fantastic debt America owes to its maritime activity," wrote *The Lookout* editor Tom Baab in 1954, "as a nation we have virtually no maritime tradition." The lessons of the two world wars pointed clearly to the wisdom of maintaining a sound merchant fleet. In both wars, the United States and her allies experienced a harrowing lack of adequate merchant shipping and paid the price in time, lives, and money. Yet,

The Reverend Dr. Raymond S. Hall with a seafarer

The Reverend Dr. Raymond S. Hall

To those who served with him in the armed forces during the Second World War, Hall was "Chappie," short for "Chaplain." After he became the first U.S. Army paratroop chaplain to actually jump with the troops — from the lead plane of the 502nd Parachute Infantry, 101st Airborne Division, landing in Normandy several hours before H-hour on D-Day, June 6, 1944 — he was the "Parachute Parson."

In his usual raucous and irreverent manner, Hall referred to himself as "Jumping Jesus."

The seafarers knew Hall's war stories by heart. How, convinced that parachute troopers wanted "fighting" chaplains, Hall parachuted with his troops behind the lines, helping everywhere he could — particularly with the wounded — until he himself received an eye injury from flying shrapnel. He recovered from his wounds in a British hospital, then took part in the September 1944 invasion of the Netherlands, this time going in by glider after doctors would not pass him for any more jumping. Captured by the Germans, he was held prisoner in Germany and Poland for four months before he was able to escape and make his way to Russia, where he finally hooked up with U.S. authorities in Odessa and was repatriated to the United States. The Army was so impressed with Hall that regular jump training was made mandatory for chaplains assigned to paratroop divisions.

At 25 South Street, Hall was known for his common sense and pithy turn-of-phrase. He called the Institute "the Church at work with its sleeves rolled up" and "the Junior United Nations" because every language was spoken there. He described his work as "befriending the men of the seven seas and helping rid the waterfront of rackets aimed at them." An old army buddy wrote of him, "Chappie refused to sit back and 'tend to his flock' within the walls of the church. He was 'relevant' and 'involved' before these words were popular."

A man who worked hard and played hard, Hall by his fiftieth birthday was troubled by a tendency to corpulence, heart problems, and a rowdy conviviality that exacerbated his health problems. Despite his popularity with the seafarers, SCI staffers, and the Institute's board of managers, Hall retired from the directorship of the Institute on May 1, 1960. Called to Trinity Episcopal Church in Portland, Maine, Hall served as rector there until 1963, when ill health forced a less active lifestyle upon him.

---

as Baab pointed out, "the Nebraska farmer, in recalling World War II, thinks not of a shortage of merchant ships but of a shortage of sugar and gasoline, inner tubes and refrigerators." And it was the Nebraska farmer who counted. In the United States in the 1950s, agriculture got space on every desk in Washington. But only a handful of American legislators were interested in maritime affairs. Seafaring was simply not one of the honored callings in the United States — as it was, for example, in Norway, where eighty-five percent of the people lived within fifteen miles of the coast. In 1955, the United States merchant marine carried only twenty-eight percent of American imports and exports, and not a single private cargo or passenger ship was scheduled for construction that year. "In war we have sunk the enemy," *Newsweek* commented. "In peace we have scuttled ourselves."[133]

At 25 South Street, a scuttled merchant marine was not the only problem. The Institute still did well those things it had always done well — supply a home away from home, care for shipwrecked crews, encourage safety at sea, provide maritime training, help find work for the unemployed, offer counseling and other chaplaincy services — but Dr. Mansfield's headquarters building, spectacular in 1913, had not kept pace with the times. A new breed of seafarer, enjoying better living conditions aboard ship, groused that the rooms at 25 South Street were too small. Others complained about the neighborhood — Lower Manhattan, once a bustling, seafaring community, had become an enclave of 350,000 office employees who dispersed at nightfall to other parts of the city or the suburbs, leaving the area lifeless except for a few policemen and the residents of the fringe of tenement houses. Seafarers no longer liked to walk to the Institute after nightfall, they said, for fear of being mugged. Furthermore, an increasing number of seamen were married and had homes to go to while in port, and many single men now had families or relatives to go home to. The crews of passenger ships had only a few hours in port and then sailed again, so they were not candidates for 25 South Street.

In 1953, architects had estimated that rehabilitation of 25 South Street would cost $3,000,000. At the same time, New York City officials began to talk of reclaiming the waterfront slum area around Coenties Slip as part of a massive redevelopment plan encompassing an area roughly bounded by Whitehall and Wall Streets, and South and Pearl Streets. The city government, when asked about the question of land acquisition for this all-encompassing project, declared that it would "invite present owners" — of which 25 South Street was one — "to participate or face condemnation under Title I of the National Housing Act." Understandably, SCI's board of managers was reluctant to undertake a $3,000,000 rehabilitation plan of a building that might soon fall under the ax of Title I condemnation.

Yet it was clear that something would have to be done about the building, and, perhaps, about the mission of the Institute itself. With that in mind, and aware that so many of the seafarers were foreigners these days, the board recommended in 1954 that the Reverend Dr. Raymond S. Hall, SCI's director, be detached from active service for about three and a half months in order to make a trip to ports around the world. Hall was charged with determining the needs of foreign seafarers in matters of housing, religious help, and social activities, and with investigating the conditions of American seafarers in foreign ports.[134] On February 18, 1954, members of the Institute's "crew" gathered on the flying bridge atop the building and waved bon voyage to their skipper, who was aboard the SS *United States* as she slid past the Battery and into the Narrows on her way to England.

Hall returned brimful of insights and suggestions, and he pressed for immediate modernization. Larger rooms were needed, he urged, each with shower and toilet. He advocated more foreign clubs for the Institute's changing constituency, and an all-weather, rooftop beer garden where cabarets and dances could be held. These improvements, Hall felt, would best serve the seafarers.

The board, however, could not agree on an appropriate course. Some members were sentimental about the Institute's glorious past and resisted change; others looked to the future and were anxious to press forward. Nudged by board president Clarence G. Michalis, who since 1950 had been advocating expansion to the various sections of the port — up the Hudson River, Hoboken, Bayonne, Brooklyn — they compromised by agreeing to more studies, pilot surveys, and reviews.

In July 1955, Captain Jørgen U. Bjørge, a Norwegian sea captain, presented Hall with an unsolicited plan by which the Institute might operate an employment agency for foreign-flag seamen. Bjørge and his wife, Jean, hoping to find shoreside work so they could settle down and start a family, had exhaustively researched the topic ashore and then typed it up at sea during one of the captain's long voyages. While the maritime unions did not approve of the proposal and vetoed it immediately, claiming employment as their own domain, Hall was so impressed with the Bjørges that he hired Jørgen as a ship visitor. Within six months, "Captain George," as he came to be known, had produced a report on foreign-flag ship visitation, which noted that an average of thirty-five ships of many nationalities arrived in the Port of New York every twenty-four hours, and about thirty-five ships sailed within the same time period. A relatively large percentage of these ships were under foreign-flag registration, manned by crews of mixed nationalities. "These ships are scattered all over New York's widespread waterfront," he wrote. "To my knowledge, very few of these vessels receive any attention or courtesy from welfare organizations or churches. . . . some definite forward steps in the field of social or welfare work on the New York waterfront are both justifiable and desirable."[135] Bjørge stressed the preparation of a special list of expected arrivals every day and the importance of visiting the ship the same day it arrived.

As Michalis had foreseen, it became impossible to ignore the fact that the "Port of New York" had sprawled over an area that now included not only Manhattan, Brooklyn, and Staten Island in New York City, but also Hoboken, Newark, Bayonne, Elizabeth, Weehawken, and Perth Amboy across the Hudson in New Jersey as well. During 1957, Hall, Bjørge, and board member Franklin E. Vilas visited sites for possible SCI expansion in Brooklyn and Port Newark, and by the end of November, Bjørge was able to record in his diary, "Mr. Vilas sounded like he wants to go ahead with plans for Port Newark."[136] Three weeks later, Hall showed Bjørge new blueprints of a proposed building in Port Newark.[137]

On January 23, 1958, Clarence G. Michalis retired after twenty-six years at the helm of SCI's board of managers, and was succeeded by Frank Vilas. (The board created the office of chairman of the board for Michalis, so that he could continue in a less active but befittingly prominent role after his many years of distinguished leadership.) Vilas, like most new presidents, was able to take advantage of the goodwill afforded him on his inauguration, and the general expectation that the new president would make some changes. The board executive committee made a concession. While certain sections of the 25 South

SINK OR SWIM

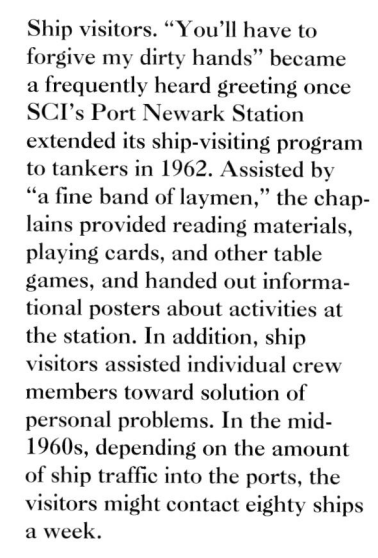

Ship visitors. "You'll have to forgive my dirty hands" became a frequently heard greeting once SCI's Port Newark Station extended its ship-visiting program to tankers in 1962. Assisted by "a fine band of laymen," the chaplains provided reading materials, playing cards, and other table games, and handed out informational posters about activities at the station. In addition, ship visitors assisted individual crew members toward solution of personal problems. In the mid-1960s, depending on the amount of ship traffic into the ports, the visitors might contact eighty ships a week.

Ship visitor Captain Bjørge in the late 1950s

85

Clarence G. Michalis

Since 1924 a member of SCI's board, from 1932 to 1957 its president, and from 1958 until 1969 its chairman, Michalis enjoyed a long, distinguished career at the Institute.

Born in Cincinnati in 1885, Michalis received an engineering degree from Stevens Institute of Technology in 1907. Soon afterward, he joined Thomas A. Edison, who intended to manufacture a new form of dry-cell battery. Edison offered Michalis a job as project manager; Michalis, however, after sizing up the project, told Edison the cell would be a failure because of the impurities in the commercial chemicals then available. "I will not stay because I am too young to be connected with a failure," he said. The battery was a failure, and Edison from then on referred to Michalis as "the damn young man who would not continue to spend my money."[138]

After World War I, Michalis entered banking. In 1933, he was elected a trustee of the Seamen's Bank for Savings; in 1943, he was named president and chairman of its board. While chief executive of the bank, he founded its fine arts collection, featuring scenes of the sea. His philanthropic and community interests were wide-ranging and far-reaching. During World War II, Michalis worked tirelessly as head of the American Relief for Holland. For this, and for his work as head of the Holland Flood Relief in 1953, he received the Grand Officer's Cross of the Order of Orange-Nassau from the Queen of the Netherlands.

Michalis's forty-five years of stewardship at the Institute spanned the Depression, World War II, and the turbulent postwar changes in shipping. Throughout these often stressful times, his guidance was instrumental. He foresaw the transformation of the Port of New York and urged his fellow board members to expand SCI's operation to Newark. "The sailor has changed as his ships have changed," he noted in a speech in 1956. With Michalis at the helm, the Institute changed to keep pace. He died on December 13, 1970.

Street building should be immediately refurbished, they said, and steps taken to promote wider use by seamen of that facility, and "while it was the consensus that our building and its location at 25 South Street were a vital part of the program and might remain so," it was also agreed that such a conclusion "did not change the need for pursuing a program to develop stations strategically located throughout the Port of New York." Pleased, Vilas immediately asked the planning committee to bring in a report on a Port Newark Station as soon as possible.[139]

In May 1958, the Institute's new International Seamen's Club opened at 25 South Street. Located on the second floor of the Institute, the new recreational facility consisted of a cafe decorated with bright blue and red checkered tablecloths, and ship's running lights affixed to the walls with dolphin brackets. An adjoining lounge provided a place where seafarers could read, rest, play cards, or chat. Hall, in his dedication speech, said, "We want this club to serve in a truly international way and we are going to make sure that it does by arranging transportation to foreign crews from the hard-to-reach areas where their ships often dock." Seafarers from five British and Scandinavian ships were brought to the opening party by special bus, inaugurating regular bus service between 25 South Street and the isolated Port Newark area. By the close of the year, the club

FRANKLIN E. VILAS

Succeeding to SCI's presidency upon the retirement of Clarence G. Michalis in 1958, Frank Vilas became a salient force molding the Institute to meet the changing needs of seafarers. He encouraged decentralization of its operation through the Port Newark Station and expanded ship-visiting services.

An employee at Con Edison who, during World War II, had been in direct charge of Manhattan's gas and electric distribution system, Vilas joined the Institute's board in 1948. Working with director John Mulligan, he was instrumental in the planning and construction of SCI's new headquarters building at 15 State Street. He also contributed tirelessly to the establishment of the Port Newark Station and lived to see it grow into the present-day International Seafarers' Center. In 1970, when he retired from Con Edison as assistant to the president for public relations, he stepped down from SCI's presidency and became chairman of the board, in which capacity he served "gently but resolutely" — as one staff member recalled — until 1980.

"Vilas was probably a real seafarer at heart," a former SCI officer reflected. After he was widowed, he lived on his trawler *Daniel Wells*, spending most of the winter in Florida waters. In June of each year, he went north, where he moved aboard *Daniel Wells Jr.*, a small sloop based in Rockland, Maine. He died on June 22, 1990, and was remembered as a "true friend of seafarers and the Institute."

Franklin Vilas with the Reverend Dr. Hall

had provided enjoyable evenings for 13,000 sailors from more than forty nations.[140]

Recognizing an additional opportunity to serve foreign seafarers, the Institute in July 1958 welcomed to 25 South Street ANGYRA, the International Society for the Aid of Greek Seamen, which converted a wartime dormitory at SCI into its new New York headquarters. Established in 1952, the agency extended personal, legal, financial, medical, and other aid to Greek seafarers, who served under many flags aboard ships owned by Greek interests.[141]

In 1958, the Port Authority of New York and New Jersey embarked upon a grand project to build multimillion-dollar terminals in Hoboken and Newark, New Jersey. Meanwhile, an $85 million, many-piered project was under construction in Brooklyn. And, the Port Authority had announced extensive new enterprises in Newark and adjacent Elizabeth. These huge pier developments offered virtually no facilities for the convenience, comfort, or recreation of seafarers. At the urging of Vilas, Hall, and Bjørge, the board executive committee determined to undertake the detailed planning necessary to establish a branch at Port Newark, "it being the sentiment that an operation there was most desirable at an early date."[142] Because Bjørge constantly stressed the importance of a place for seafarers to play soccer, the board decided to focus in

Seafarer playing soccer. The regulation-size soccer field became so popular with seafarers they scrimmaged on it even when it was snow-covered. The addition of stadium lights in 1962 extended the playing time. At the dedication of SCI Mariners Center Newark, the field was renamed the W. Lawrence McLane Sports Field in memory of the board member who had worked so tirelessly to envision and execute plans for the Port Newark Station.

particular on the establishment of a sports field with limited facilities.

As the decade ended, word came that the taking of land for the Battery Park North development, which included 25 South Street, would begin for certain toward the end of 1961. The Institute, for the first time in its history, faced an uncertain future. SCI would have to expand, consolidate, relocate, and change its mission substantially to meet the changing needs of a "new" breed of seafarers, fewer of whom were American or Christian.

A board member, John H.G. Pell, speaking at a meeting in 1959, summed it up:

"We are in a period of incredible difficulties," he said.

In April 1960, when the Seamen's Church Institute signed a twenty-year lease with the Port Authority for land on which to build an athletic field and a modest, single-story, recreation building, the authority was approaching the halfway mark in its multi-purpose $400,000,000 marine terminal program. Six new terminals in the Port Newark, Elizabeth, Brooklyn, and Hoboken areas were opened during that year, to great fanfare. Two new cargo distribution centers were completed and construction was started on six additional structures of this type. Existing depots handled seven million tons of cargo valued at $3.7 billion.

At Port Newark, a new, open, three-berth, $3,645,000 terminal and a new Waterfront Commission hiring center were begun.

But a seafarer arriving there encountered a barren concrete landscape of 640 acres, where he or she could not buy a newspaper or postage stamp, post a letter, or get a cup of coffee.

Thus, there was a great deal of anticipation in May when board member W. Lawrence McLane, chairman of the committee on special services for seamen, announced that work on a soccer field for seafarers had begun at the corner of Calcutta and Export Streets. By October, the field was ready for its first game and dedication services. Two hundred fifty people, including the Right Reverend Horace W.B. Donegan, bishop of the Diocese of New York, boarded the Hudson River Day Liner *Knickerbocker* in Manhattan and motored to Port Newark. As the liner pulled into Pier 14, the Institute was officially welcomed to the port by the suffragan bishop of Newark, the vice chairman of the Port of New York Authority, and the opposing soccer teams of seafarers, who waved the flags of their respective countries. The Merchant Marine Academy band and the teams led the group on a half-mile march from the ship to the field, where Bishop Donegan laid the cornerstone for the recreation building with the same trowel used nearly fifty years earlier at the dedication of 25 South Street. Board president Franklin Vilas kicked out the first ball.

The Seamen's Church Institute had arrived in Port Newark.

Eight months later, on June 15, 1961, while the international code flags QFK — welcome — flapped in the breeze, more than one hundred fifty visitors witnessed SCI's first stage of expansion at the dedication ceremonies of the Port Newark Station. Port Authority Commissioner James C. Kellogg 3d, along with consuls from Norway, Great Britain, Colombia, Germany, and the Netherlands,

SINK OR SWIM

The original Port Newark Station building. By 1961, Port Newark had grown to the extent that it was now the main import center in the nation for frozen meats and foreign automobiles. On July 17, 1961, the Institute opened the first building of a three-part building plan for its Port Newark Station. The new building, designed as a sports facility, also provided a snack bar, lounge, showers, and dressing rooms and could accommodate about seventy-five sailors.

The enlarged Port Newark Station, rechristened the Seamen's Church Institute Mariners Center Newark. Overcrowding of the original one-story building, which opened in 1961, soon prompted SCI's board of managers to construct a second, larger building, connected to the original by an enclosed walkway. Inside, the great expanses of glass gave the feeling of lightness and warmth, as did the finishes of terrazzo, teakwood, and textured plaster. The additional 11,850 square feet of interior space permitted SCI, by the end of 1965, to offer at Port Newark many of the services to seafarers formerly available only at 25 South Street in Manhattan, including dances with live music, social evenings, educational classes in art and music appreciation, and film programs.

89

CREW OF THE *ANDREA DORIA* IN FRONT OF THE INSTITUTE

On July 25, 1956, the opulent Italian luxury liner *Andrea Doria* collided in the fog with the smaller Swedish-American cruise ship *Stockholm* sixty miles off Nantucket Shoals Lightship. During the next eleven hours, 1,662 of the *Doria*'s 1,706 passengers and crew were rescued from the stricken ship. Then the *Doria* rolled bottom up, thrust her propellers into the air, and plunged to the ocean floor.

When news of the disaster reached the Institute, seafarers pitched in to help SCI staffers prepare ditty bags containing cigarettes, stationery, razors, toothpaste, combs, and other toilet articles. Tired and unshaven, seventy-five crew members from the *Doria* arrived at SCI, having lost their ship, their belongings, and their jobs to the savage bow of the *Stockholm*.

The Institute had further opportunity to help victims of the disaster when, on November 7, 1956, the Federal Court, faced with a space problem and the prospect of massive and prolonged testimony involving more than $50,000,000 in claims, transferred pre-trial hearings on the collision to a room at the Institute's Marine Museum.[143]

The sinking of the *Titanic* in 1912 had led to the first International Conference on the Safety of Life at Sea, and the *Doria-Stockholm* collision also had positive repercussions. The Swedish-American Line assigned two officers to every bridge watch instead of one. Radar manufacturers increased the tempo of their work to produce a new type of radar that would show the true motion of other ships instead of their relative positions. And the House Merchant Marine Committee appointed a special subcommittee to investigate the safety problem of ships at sea.[144]

THE *IDEAL-X*

The *Ideal-X* carried the first shipment of Sea-Land containers from Newark to Houston in 1956. In that year, Malcolm McLean, president of an enterprising New Jersey trucking company that would later become Sea-Land, inaugurated the era of ocean-borne intermodal containerization with a World War II vintage T-2 tanker he had modified. Hoping to minimize cargo handling and reduce the opportunities for theft and damage, McLean lifted fifty-eight truck trailers off their bodies, loaded them onto the spar deck of the *Ideal-X*, and sent the ship on a four-day voyage from Newark to Houston. The event passed almost unnoticed, even when four workers offloaded the cargo in Houston in just two days. But it would revolutionize the shipping industry.

stood by as the Right Reverend Leland Stark, bishop of the Diocese of Newark, dedicated the new building. After the dedication, crew members from the Grancolombian Lines *Ciudad de Pasto* and the Norwegian ship MS *Havhok* kicked the ball in the first game of the season on the new sports field. The game ended in a friendly tie: 1-1.

The Port Newark Station officially opened on Monday, July 17, 1961, at 3 P.M. The first two visitors hailed from the British MS *Bristol City*, reported Captain Bjørge, newly appointed supervisor of Ships Visiting International. During the first week, Bjørge reported that most of the men "had their refreshments and watched TV"; President Kennedy's TV speech to the nation drew a particularly large audience, he noted. Others bought stamps, mailed letters, and purchased magazines, newspapers, and maps. "But I believe the most interesting comment came from a stewardess on board the British freighter SS *Albano*," Bjørge wrote later. "In the guest book she wrote the following: 'I wish to express my sincere appreciation. . . . I am also proud to be the first stewardess to find comfort and relaxation here.' (Signed) Mrs. Judy McCleir, SS *Albano*, Ellerman Line, Hull, England."[145]

In 1962, the Port Authority dedicated the first section of its $150,000,000 Port Elizabeth pier complex on the new Elizabeth Channel, south of Port

Newark on Newark Bay, bringing to a close the first phase of its ambitious, 703-acre Port Elizabeth-Port Newark development. That year, SCI pioneered its equally ambitious tanker project; ship visitors based at the Port Newark Station extended their service to oil tankers stationed at remote berths as far away as Weehawken, Staten Island, and Perth Amboy. These crews were among the most isolated of all seafarers, since tankers fell into the category of ships that berth great distances from any populous waterfront area, often at most inaccessible places, because of their dangerous and flammable cargo. The Reverend G. Basil Hollas, a native of Halifax, Yorkshire, was added to SCI's staff to assist in the development of the tanker program, as was Greek-born Basile Tzanakis, who was fluent in Greek, Italian, Arabic, and Spanish. The year 1962 also saw the first time SCI chaplains conducted religious services for the crews aboard foreign-flag ships during the Christmas holidays.

By the end of the year, the Institute's board of managers was ready to proceed with the second stage of construction at Port Newark and chose George W. Clark Associates of Manhattan as architect. The new three-story structure, with portable walls that could be moved to change the sizes of rooms for various activities, would add an aesthetic asset to the sprawling 640 acres of nondescript Port Newark warehouses — and would still provide the only social and recreational outlet for seafarers in the area. Construction continued through 1964 and much of 1965 (unexpectedly, a near-ground-level water table hindered preparation of the site and prevented the hoped-for spring 1965 opening), and toward the final stages, *The Lookout* editor reported that "seamen from every maritime country left nose prints on the glass expanses of the building," but by November 1965, the new building was ready for dedication. Officially renamed the Seamen's Church Institute Mariners Center Newark, the enlarged premises

WOMEN AT SEA

In 1955, the Coast Guard estimated that fewer than a fraction of one percent of the jobs on ships went to women. Women worked as stewardesses, nurses, children's attendants, waitresses, assistant pursers, social directors, salesgirls, beauticians, physiotherapists, telephone operators, and florists. They were not hired as ordinary or able-bodied seafarers, except in the Soviet Union, where there had been able-bodied seawomen for some time. The Scandinavian countries sometimes employed women as seagoing radio operators — much to the bemusement of the male "Sparks" of other nations.

While men who went to sea were frequently loners, women did so because they enjoyed working with people. Typical of many was seafarer Evelyn MacQuarrie, who, in the early 1950s, was one of two social hostesses on the *Ile de France*'s popular Caribbean cruises. MacQuarrie's job was to make sure that everyone had a wonderful time. *The Lookout* editor Faye Hammel described it: "This involved everything from seeing that Miss Jones met the good-looking young man at the third-table-from-the-left, to giving a lecture on shopping in Cuba, to listening to the troubles of the chronic complainer who's come on this cruise to get away from it all."[146]

The first female seafarer to appear in the Institute's records was an unnamed stewardess who showed up at 25 South Street one day in 1932, waving her discharge papers and asking to have her teeth fixed at SCI's dental clinic. SCI staffers, momentarily nonplussed, recovered and escorted her to the clinic.

were promptly christened the "Harbor Hilton" by the crew of a British freighter, the MV *Canopic*.

While the Institute put down new roots in Port Newark, board and staff members also considered the future of their headquarters operation in Manhattan. Under the leadership of the Reverend John M. Mulligan, who succeeded Raymond Hall as SCI's director in 1960, the consensus emerged that a new headquarters building was needed.

Important to any long-range planning at SCI were the development strategies of the Downtown Association, which early in 1962 abandoned plans to build apartments in the immediate area of 25 South Street, thus lifting the threat of Title I condemnation. The Institute's board, if it chose, could raze the building and rebuild on the same site. Or it could sell and move to another site. Meanwhile, the New York Stock Exchange was considering a site just south of the Institute — a move that would substantially enhance property values in the area — and SCI's board considered it inexpedient to make any final decision to sell or lease 25 South Street until the Stock Exchange made its own final determination. So strong was this perceived symbiosis with the Stock Exchange that the Institute hired the engineering consultants, reviewed their reports, chose a site for a new headquarters building, acquired the land for it (9, 11, 12, and 17 State Street, and 10 Pearl Street), selected an architect, demolished the buildings on the new site, and prepared a carefully worded advertisement that the property at 25 South Street would soon become available — yet postponed the entertainment of bids for the sale until the Stock Exchange showed its hand. Finally, on October 18, 1965, with a bid from Percy Uris and his brother for $2,600,000, the board resolved to sell the historic building at 25 South Street. (In May of the following year, the Stock Exchange gave up all plans to relocate to Broad Street.)

During the 1960s, America's increasing involvement in Vietnam drew ships and seafarers from the East to the West Coast. Because of this, and because the hub of maritime activity remaining in New York City had long since shifted to Port Elizabeth and Port Newark, the occupancy rate at 25 South Street reached

ALCOHOLIC SEAFARERS

The Institute pioneered in coping with alcoholism on the waterfront in 1945 when its Department of Special Services developed the first therapy program among the seamen's agencies. Headed by William J. Fowler, himself a recovering alcoholic and former seafarer, the Institute's Alcoholics Assistance Bureau soon was lauded for its realistic and effective approach.

In 1954, a special club room adjoining the new third-floor offices of the Alcoholics Assistance Bureau marked an important addition to the Institute's facilities for aiding alcoholic seafarers. The large, newly furnished room was designed to serve as a refuge and haven for men who were in the early, difficult stages of sobriety. Counselors from the bureau aided them in getting past the small problems that might otherwise make them dash for a bottle.

The Reverend Dr. John M. Mulligan

Having served as a clerical vice president on SCI's board of managers for nine years, Mulligan, rector of All Angels Church in Manhattan since 1947, was an old hand when he became director of the Institute in 1960.

Described by a contemporary as a "big, husky, full-faced guy" who was a "real leader," Mulligan guided the Institute through troubled times of reorganization, consolidation, and redefinition. Under his capable direction, the Port Newark Station was conceived and established, 25 South Street was sold, and the new headquarters building at 15 State Street was erected.

In addition to his duties at the Institute, Mulligan was active in the community of New York City at large. While at All Angels, he published *Toward City Conservation*, a book written in memorandum form that proposed a multifaceted government and a neighborhood approach to cleaning up the city and preventing slums. He was one of the founders of the League of West Side Organizations, where he acted as co-chairman for a number of years.

Mulligan retired in 1977 but remained an honorary member of the board of managers until his death on August 25, 1991.

---

a very low ebb in the summer of 1966. Then came news that the National Maritime Union would soon build high-rise apartment buildings for its membership. These factors combined to convince Vilas that any SCI hotel operation in downtown Manhattan should be on a very modest scale indeed. Some board members felt that if SCI were going to build a new building in lower Manhattan, it should not be a hotel at all. But offering seafarers a place to sleep was so much a part of what SCI did, and had always done, that this service was retained. The new building plans incorporated a five-story base that would house social, religious, recreational, educational, and eating facilities, and an eighteen-story hotel that would accommodate about 340 persons. Modernity did bring about one revolutionary change: For the first time women crew members and seamen's wives would be admitted to the sleeping quarters.

On October 20, 1966, SCI went public with its plans for a new headquarters building. In an announcement issued to the New York area news media, "The world's largest shore center for merchant seamen, Seamen's Church Institute of New York," declared a "phase of renewal and modernization" — just as it had done periodically since its founding more than a century and a quarter earlier. Indeed, the 1966 board of managers might well have explained the rationale for its action in precisely the same terms used by its predecessors in 1868 when acquiring land for the North River Station:

> This metropolis is peculiar to rapid changes — everything must yield to the necessities of the living present, with little lingering respect for the old landmarks or time-hallowed associations. So now we turn to the future with bright anticipation of increased means for usefulness in new, commodious and substantial quarters.[147]

In some ways the Institute was simply swept up in the 1960s mania for urban renewal. As construction commenced on the new building at 15 State Street, the foundation excavation became one of a series of huge holes in the ground along the Battery from the Custom House to Coenties Slip, where nine skyscrapers and five new superblocks were being built — and this in addition to the sixteen-acre World Trade Center underway on the Hudson River and the fifteen-acre Brooklyn Bridge Southwest urban-renewal project. Sadly, lower Manhattan, the last stronghold of the small, historic structures that served the early 19th-century's sailing age, was virtually wiped out — perhaps an appropriate metaphor for the sea changes in the shipping industry confronting the Institute. And perhaps it was fitting, too, that the two-foot cornerstone from the old building had to be shaved down to four inches square so it would fit into the narrow walls of the new building.[148]

On December 8, 1967, while construction workers shouted and hoisting equipment groaned, the cornerstone from 25 South Street was rededicated and reinstalled at 15 State Street, with a 1967 engraving added to the original 1912 engraving.

Thus the old gave way to the new.

In early 1968, the Institute began its move to 15 State Street. While the transfer was a mere four blocks in actual distance, the move was wrenching for staff members and seafarers alike. Particularly upset were retired seafarers who had become permanent residents of 25 South Street; only seamen discharged from a ship within six months would be eligible to live in the new building. "The closing of the doors of 25 South Street did not take place without an expression of deep mourning and deep sorrow registered by one seaman in the name of seamen of the Seven Seas," reported one eyewitness bitterly. "He awaited the deadline of 4 p.m., having been entrusted with the keys of the building which were to be turned over to the wrecking company officials. Pain was visible on his face . . . . [He was] murmuring 'This never should have happened — the poor guys are scattered all over — State Street is a hotel — not a home for seamen.'"[149] The Institute, it was said, had treated these men harshly.

So vociferous were the charges, Mulligan felt called upon to publish a rebuttal. "While it was true that a number of retired seafarers were allowed to stay in the South Street building after they had reached inactive status, the Institute was never originally chartered or intended as a permanent 'home' for seamen," Mulligan wrote in an article in the *Villager*. Their continued stay was permitted because of the availability of extra rooms and out of consideration for their past sea service. All retired seamen who were residing in the building were notified months in advance that they could not expect accommodations in the new building, and a social worker and chaplain helped these elderly men to relocate to suitable quarters.[150]

Another casualty of the move was the Institute's museum, after fifteen years of exhibition on the third floor of 25 South Street. The collection, assembled informally over the years, consisted of models made by seafarers, donations from

15 State Street

"Since it was founded in 1834, the Seamen's Church Institute of New York has carried on its program in over a dozen different buildings on the waterfront," the Reverend John M. Mulligan, SCI's director, explained in 1966 when he announced plans for a new headquarters building. "As conditions relating to seamen have changed, the program of the Institute has changed to minister to the present need.... In each era, the Institute has seen to it that an appropriate building was provided so that its program could function effectively."

The triangular building site at State and Pearl Streets, which had once been part of an old Dutch fort, dictated the shape of the new building. The architects, Eggers and Higgins, achieved a roughly triangular form somewhat suggestive of a ship's bow.

The massive (thirty-five feet high from roof to tip), poured-concrete Christian cross at the top of the Seamen's Church Institute State Street building was completed in late November 1967, and the illumination for night lighting was installed in mid-December. Constructing and bracing the wooden form for the cross presented a bone-chilling challenge to the carpenters working in biting winds 277 feet above the ground.

shipping lines and other businesses, and gifts from foreign governments. While valuable pieces were retained, the rest was sold at auction. The Institute also gave up its rooftop lighthouse beacon and time ball that made the 25 South Street building a famous landmark; both were donated to the projected South Street Seaport Museum. Other historic items, such as the Sir Galahad figurehead, the bell from the *Atlantic*, and many of the bronze or brass memorial plaques, were lovingly transported from 25 South Street to 15 State Street and installed in their new home.

On May 28, 1968, the chapel at 15 State Street was dedicated, and "the good ship *Institute*, replete with fo'c'sle, galleys and twenty-three decks," opened its facilities to a host of admiring seafarers and landlubbers, among them a reviewer from the *New York Times*, who reported that the operation, particularly the hotel, had "none of the charitable-institution atmosphere" so obvious at 25 South Street.[151] In comparison to the old building, which had 795 rooms at the time of its closing, the new hotel offered 295 rooms, fifty of them doubles, and all with private bath.

"The Institute is changing," said Mulligan at the time.

He might have added that the Institute, with its usual aplomb, had overcome its period of difficulties.

Sir Galahad moves to 15 State Street. The famous figurehead, whose origin never became entirely clear, was given to SCI in 1927 by I.J. Merritt in memory of his father. For many years mounted over the entrance to 25 South Street, Sir Galahad was given a prominent place of honor in the new building.

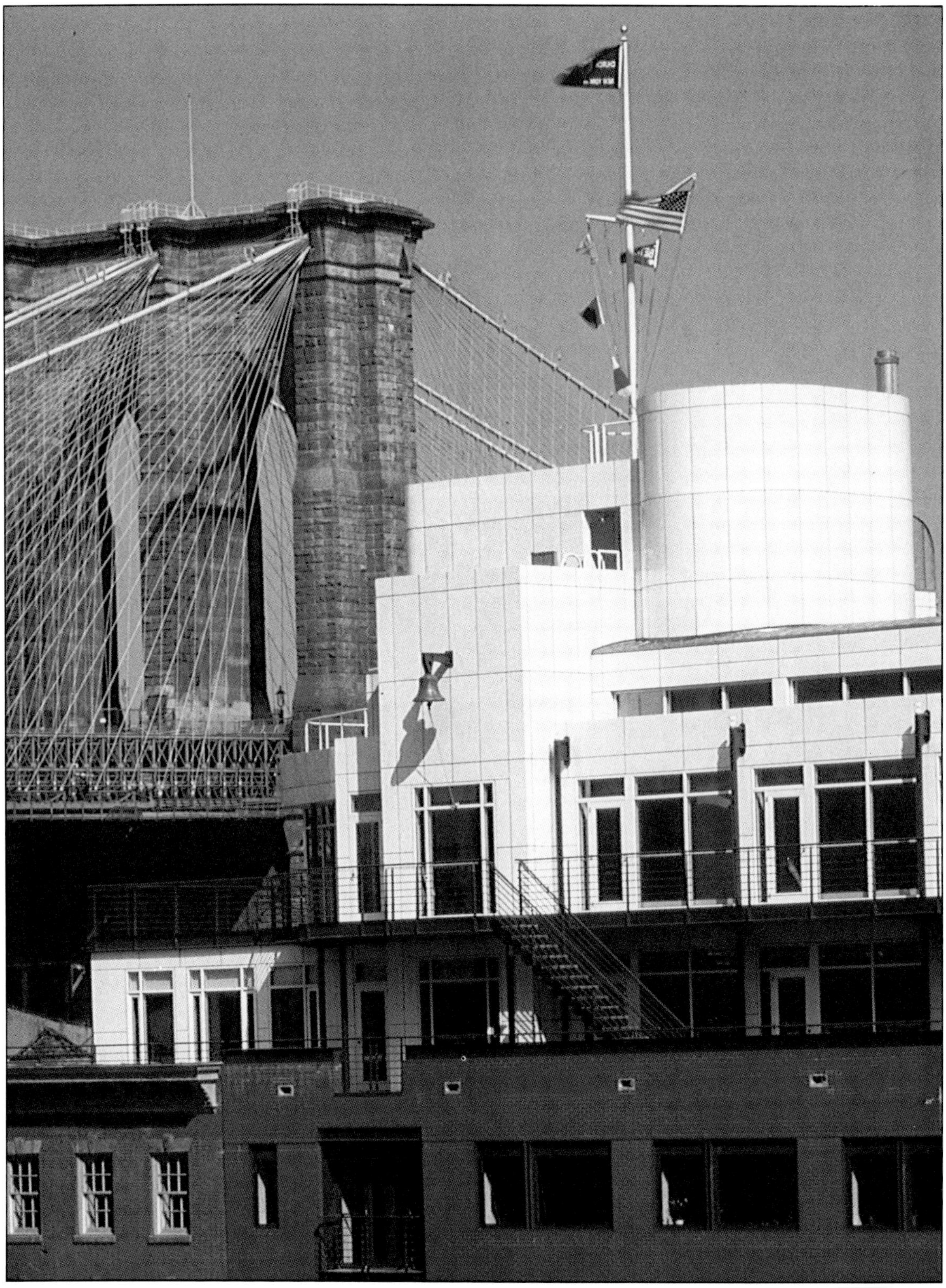

CHAPTER SEVEN

Sea Changes

On December 12, 1986, the German-built freighter *Court Carrier* limped into New York Harbor with 2,000 tons of Portland cement. An engine explosion had disabled the vessel off Cape Hatteras, and because the cargo was two weeks late, the buyer refused it. Unable to reach the owner — no one seemed to know who the owner was — and with no money for repairs, the ship's captain, his wife, and a crew of sixteen (from Colombia, Chile, and Peru) were stranded aboard the ship at Pier 7 in Brooklyn.

The Reverend Dr. Paul K. Chapman, director of SCI's Center for Seafarers' Rights, thought the owner, in all probability, had abandoned the ship because he could no longer pay the bills. The shipping industry was in dire straits, Chapman explained, and "you bump into ships like this all the time all around the world. 'Abandon ship' used to mean to get off the ship. Now it is a term used by owners to get away from their debts."[152]

Indeed, the *Court Carrier*'s plight was all too common. In 1985, shipowners, crews, brokers, and bankers worldwide were hit by a typhoon of foreclosures, bankruptcy proceedings, and write-downs because of plunging freight rates and ship values. The problems of shipping seemed deeper and more widespread than ever — the most severe upheaval in shipping since the Depression, some claimed. Hundreds of surplus ships were moored in vast floating parking lots off Piraeus, Greece, in Norwegian fjords, and in the Bay of Brunei. As a reporter at the time explained, "Like other business busts, this one traces its origins to an earlier boom. Visions of a trade bonanza in oil in the early 1970s and in other commodities 10 years later encouraged shipowners to enlarge their fleets and led banks to compete with each other to finance the building. But both expansions fizzled, leaving the world merchant fleet a quarter larger than was necessary."[153]

Fortunately, staffers at the Seamen's Church Institute, keeping pace with

SCI's new headquarters at 241 Water Street won the American Institute of Architects' 1991 Award for Design Excellence and received a Citation for Architectural Design from the New York City Landmarks Preservation Commission. The same year, it also received praise from *Time* magazine for Best of Design and *Interiors* magazine for Best in Institutional Design.

99

Sir Galahad in place at 241 Water Street

these changes in shipping, had developed a strategy for situations like that of the abandoned crew of the *Court Carrier*. A lien could be slapped on the ship in order to recover the back wages owed to the crew. Next, if the owner was not forthcoming, the court could auction the ship and cargo to recover the back wages. (U.S. law protected seafarers' wages.) Third, SCI staffers could advance repatriation money so that the crew could go home while awaiting the completion of lengthy legal proceedings. And when the case was finally settled, SCI would forward the recovered wages to the crew.

To ease the crew's immediate problems, the Institute and the Roman Catholic port chaplain from the Stella Maris Seamen's Center in Brooklyn raised $400 to keep the *Court Carrier*'s stranded crew in food. Sidney Kalban, an attorney from the Manhattan firm of Phillips and Cappiello (lawyers for the National Maritime Union), was hired, and, assisted by an SCI attorney, he petitioned the U.S. Marshal to seize the *Court Carrier*. This accomplished, the ship was auctioned in May 1986. Although the beleaguered crew members did not receive their full back pay, which amounted to more than $200,000, the lawyers were satisfied when the crew got slightly more than half that.

That the Seamen's Church Institute should be dealing with matters of law at all was a recent innovation. At the turn of the century, the Institute had had a large hand in forcing legislation on behalf of seafarers' rights. During those days, the Seamen's Branch of the Legal Aid Society operated out of SCI's Mission House at 34 Pike Street. When the building at 25 South Street was completed in 1912, however, SCI and the Legal Aid Society went separate ways. Seafarers could still find assistance at the Legal Aid Society when they needed it, but the Seamen's Branch was no longer housed in the Institute's building.

In the late 1970s, SCI again turned its attention to the legal rights of seafarers. The Reverend Francis C. Huntington, SCI's deputy director, estimated in 1979 that more than 300,000 seafarers came into the Port of New York and New Jersey every year; that eighty percent were foreigners; and that "three-fourths of them are from developing countries, are low paid and lead marginal existences."[154] Because of serious unemployment in their home countries, growing numbers of these men and women were willing to be hired regardless of contract, salary, or ship. Moreover, as developing nations competed to place their citizens on foreign-flag vessels, laws of those nations developed to protect employment rather than the employee. In a throw-back to conditions that prevailed in shipping more than a century earlier, abuse of seafarers became rampant.

These abuses were all too apparent to SCI's ship visitors, who in the years since the establishment of SCI's International Seafarers' Center in Port Newark/Port Elizabeth had become the vanguard of the Institute's mission to seafarers. More and more, the problems seafarers wished to discuss with the Institute's chaplains concerned employment — so much so, in fact, that the chaplains began to redefine their ministry. By 1979, the Reverend George Dawson, senior chaplain at the International Seafarers' Center, had come to

An aerial view of the Greater Port of New York-New Jersey

consider "labor troubleshooter" on foreign ships to be part of his portfolio.[155] Dawson had a lot of trouble to shoot. The withholding of compensation and benefits, excessive duty hours, false or broken contracts, illegal termination, denial of right to counsel, subhuman living conditions, and disregard for safety standards aboard ship were all common areas of abuse.

Yet Dawson and the other chaplains found that they were ill-prepared for this expansion of responsibility. Solving employment problems called for specialized skills. Moreover, as Paul Chapman put it, "We were tired of [figuratively] pulling the seafarers out of the water. We wanted to go up the river and find out who was throwing them in."[156]

Out of these incentives was born SCI's Center for Seafarers' Rights. Created to provide a central source for research, education, and assistance with the problems of seafarers' legal rights, and to work with the international maritime community to eliminate abuses, the center opened in early 1982. In concert with sister ship visiting agencies around the world, SCI began to collect information in a systematic way to help identify those particular ships, owners, agents, ports, and flag countries that ignored basic human rights in their merchant marine policies and practices.[157] Individual cases could be extremely complicated, as Chapman illustrated with a sketch of a typical scenario: "Just imagine a ship with a multinational crew, on which there is one seafarer who is the only national of a given country — Sri Lanka, for example. The laws, even the language of the nation under which the ship sails, are foreign to him. His captain is from still another country, the ship's owner from another yet, and the ship travels between the shores of two other nations. Six different nations are involved somehow in the work of this seafarer. If questions of his rights should arise, to whom can he turn? In fact, would he even know what his rights are?"[158]

Sometimes, indeed, seafarers had no legal rights at all. To fill these legislative gaps, SCI determined to work with foreign governments, intergovernmental agencies, and human rights and maritime groups around the world. "Clearly, we can't do this job by ourselves," Chapman said shortly after the Center for Seafarers' Rights was inaugurated. "We see ourselves as a kind of leaven seeking to affect the rest of the industry."[159] Two important international groups during the 1980s were the International Christian Maritime Association (ICMA), founded in 1969 after a number of Christian seafarer groups from throughout the world expressed the desire to work together more closely, and the International Council of Seamen's Agencies (ICOSA).

Tireless in his dedication to the improvement of conditions for Third-World seafarers, Chapman was considered overzealous by those shipowners who meticulously observed labor laws and enjoyed good relations with their crews — and who resented Chapman's failure to distinguish between them and "bad" shipowners. The relationship between Chapman and shipowner representatives on SCI's board of managers became strained, and Chapman and the Institute came to a parting of the ways. In September, 1990, Douglas B. Stevenson succeeded Chapman as director of SCI's Center for Seafarers' Rights.

An attorney and retired Coast Guard commander, Stevenson had been seconded by the Coast Guard to the State Department, and he had worked as a diplomat on the staff of the U.S. Mission to the United Nations. There he was

Passenger ship terminal. "Calling home is one of their few luxuries," says the Reverend Barbara Crafton of the seafarers who work the passenger ships that dock on Manhattan's West Side. To provide for this simple human need, SCI and the Port Authority opened the Seafarers' Center at the passenger ship terminal in the mid-1980s. In 1993, the center, says Crafton, was "AT&T's biggest customer"; seafarers made 8,060 phone calls there.

DOUGLAS B. STEVENSON

Director of the Center for Seafarers' Rights, Doug Stevenson is the mainstay of the Institute's mission to provide legal aid services for both individual seafarers and entire ships' crews.

"I would describe my work in three general areas," he says, ticking the items off on his fingers. "First, we provide free legal aid to seafarers who cannot afford counsel to aid them with work-related problems. We also provide legal advice to port chaplains around the world. Second, we provide education, to both seafarers and port chaplains. We print booklets and pamphlets to advise seafarers or to acquaint them with their rights and obligations, and we conduct workshops for port chaplains. Third, we are advocates. We are not satisfied with trying to solve the day-to-day problems that come across our desks; we want to look to the source of problems and see if we can be an influence for change. We want to improve the laws that regulate international standards and business practices that affect the lives of seafarers."

To accomplish the work of the center, Stevenson looks to government and to national regulatory agencies. He also seeks the cooperation of shipowners — many of whom, he has found, "are very responsive to our concerns." But the key to the strength of the Center for Seafarers' Rights, he believes, is the existing international network of port chaplains. "Chaplains see the insides of ships that few outsiders see, and they are told of problems that many seafarers won't even reveal to their own shipmates."

A man of keen intelligence who seasons a serious outlook on life with vivacious humor, Stevenson joined the Institute in 1990 upon retirement from the United States Coast Guard, after twenty years of service. While in the Coast Guard he was involved in strategic planning, including negotiating U.S. positions at the United Nations on law-of-the-sea, arms control, and the environment.

involved in strategic planning, including negotiating U.S. positions on law-of-the-sea, arms control, and the environment. A conciliator by nature who advocates the ombudsman approach, Stevenson soon mended the rifts — imagined or otherwise — between the Center for Seafarers' Rights and shipowner representatives on the board. "The board and the shipowner representatives on the Board fully understand that the industry is strengthened by good standards and safe ships," he says. "And good companies realize that even in the best-run companies there are going to be problems from time to time that require special attention. Here we come in as the ombudsman. The shipowners understand that we are there representing the best interests of the seafarer, but that we also realize there's a business to be run."

With the encouragement and guidance of board members Ralph Smith and George Benjamin, Stevenson took charge of the Center for Seafarers' Rights with a firm hand. Soon he was conducting seafarers' rights workshops for port chaplains in Houston, Norfolk, and Newark. He flew to Korea, Taiwan, and Japan to promote improved conditions for international crews on fishing vessels. He intervened in a case where the United States overstepped its jurisdiction to prosecute crime on a foreign ship on the high seas, and charges against a seafarer

The Reverend Jean R. Smith

As SCI's director of Seafarers' Services Division and of the Institute's International Seafarers' Center in Port Newark, the Reverend Jean Smith wears several hats.

She deftly balances the managerial aspects of her administrative job with those of ministering to the spiritual and human needs of the seafaring men and women who look to the Institute for support. Along with the three other ministers she supervises, she visits ships. She directs the International Training Center for Maritime Ministry (ITC), introducing the interns to the myriad intricacies of port chaplaincy. Often she is at the Newark center until late in the evening, welcoming the seafarers and explaining what SCI can do for them. The Port Newark center and the Seamen's Church Institute, she emphasizes, provide more than hospitality. That's the role of the USO. "But we are different by virtue of the fact that, while we provide hospitality — and that's important — we are also a religious mission. This creates an overarching context for our work."

Like many women priests, Smith came to the ministry as a second career. She was a wife and mother when she went to seminary, and she had been a speech therapist for fourteen years. After ordination in 1980, she worked in a parish in Princeton, New Jersey, for ten years. But, Smith says, "I wanted very much to work with people from developing nations or people who were a little less fortunate." In 1990, while casting about for a new church, she bumped into Jim Whittemore, then director of the Institute, at a continuing education conference. He invited her to visit the Institute. "It was instant!" Smith laughs. "I loved it immediately!"

An intense woman with a focused pastoral gaze, Smith brims with ideas for the future. Among these is working to rebuild a base of volunteers to support and participate in the center's work. She wants to reconnect the center with local congregations as a place for them to exercise their ministries.

"We are limited in our work only by our imaginations," she says.

---

were dropped. Under his direction, SCI's legal staff helped gain the release of the crews of two Taiwanese fishing vessels seized by armed rebels in Somalia.

In June 1993, the growing international problem of human smuggling landed on New York's shore when the tramp steamer *Golden Venture* ran aground off Rockaway Beach, New York, carrying hundreds of illegal Chinese immigrants. The Indonesian and Burmese crew members were arrested for their alleged role in the smuggling. But, according to Stevenson, the crew was as much a victim of the illegal smuggling rings as was the ship's human cargo. "These crime rings use throwaway ships and crews to accomplish their illicit trade," he commented. "They register their ships in countries with lax laws to avoid inspections, and they hire crew members from poor countries who are as desperate for work as are the passengers."

The Reverend Dr. James R. Whittemore

A member of the Institute's board of managers since 1970, Whittemore became its director in 1977, at a time of great transformation for the maritime industry and for the Institute — "sea changes," as he later called it.

During his fifteen years in office, Whittemore oversaw the financial reorganization of the Institute, kept a steady helm as the entire maritime industry weathered the most devastating depression since the Great Depression, guided SCI through the discontinuation of the Institute's hotel service, and supervised the sale of 15 State Street and the building of the new headquarters and Seafarers' Center on Water Street. During his eventful tenure the Institute solidified its reputation as an esteemed international resource for other agencies serving seafarers. While the Institute had provided nautical training and license preparation for many years, Whittemore expanded its program to include training courses in fire fighting, cruise-ship safety and automatic radar plotting, among other educational programs. Particularly zealous in the cause of safety at sea, he was awarded the 1992 RAdm. Halert C. Shepheard Award for achievement in marine safety by the American Bureau of Shipping & Affiliated Companies.

An engaging man whose mild manner sometimes masks a sharp mind and keen management skills, Whittemore is a graduate of Yale University and the Episcopal Divinity School and was a Harvard University Merrill Fellow in 1965. He also holds the degrees of Master of Sacred Theology and Doctor of Ministry from New York Theological Seminary. He was ordained in 1951. Prior to accepting the call as director of SCI, he was rector of Trinity Church in Princeton and a canon of Trinity Cathedral in Trenton. His earlier ministries included churches in Michigan and Massachusetts.

As a naval officer in World War II and shortly thereafter, he served aboard LSTs with assignments ranging from deck officer to commanding officer. A member of the prestigious Cruising Club of America, Whittemore is an avid blue-water sailor and has competed in the Newport Bermuda Race, among others, sailing his thirty-four-foot sloop, *The Goodly Fere*.

He retired from the Institute in September 1992.

The Reverend Barbara C. Crafton

As vicar of the new ecumenical chapel at 241 Water Street, Port Missioner Barbara C. Crafton has been charged with bringing together the two communities the Institute serves: the maritime community and the lower Manhattan community. There is much, Crafton feels, that these two communities have in common. "Ships run well despite the many cultural, religious, and even dietetic differences of the merchant seafarers who operate them. SCI has a lot to share with New York in that way. The multicultural issues that SCI deals with regularly make us a natural partner in helping parents raise loving, tolerant children in a city where racial issues are among most devastating social problems," she points out.

No stranger to SCI or lower Manhattan, Crafton, known as "Mother" Crafton since she was first called that by seafarers who thought she must be a nun, rejoined the SCI staff in 1991 after two years of service to Trinity Church in lower Manhattan. From 1983 to 1990, she was director of the Seafarers' Services Division at the Institute's International Seafarers' Center in Port Newark, where she was instrumental in setting up the Asian/North American Pastoral Training Program (now the International Training Center for Workplace Ministry) and in developing many of the programs now in place. As port missioner, Crafton continues in SCI's traditional chaplaincy to provide the services the Institute has always provided. "Although the industry has moved east, we still counsel weekly sixty to seventy-five American seafarers at our Water Street building," she says. "We assist them with housing, food, loans, references for medical attention — this work has not disappeared, although it has changed since Mansfield's time."

An astute woman with a lively wit, Crafton also serves as chaplain to the Edwin J. O'Hara Chapter of the American Merchant Marine Veterans, now headquartered in SCI's Water Street building, a chapter she was instrumental in founding. She is the author of numerous articles on her work with seafarers and a book of essays, *The Sewing Room*.

Eric K. Larsson

"The job of piloting a vessel, or standing watch on a vessel, is not easy," says Eric Larsson, who as director of SCI's Center for Maritime Education oversees a ship simulator laboratory that boasts some of the most sophisticated equipment available. "Training and lifelong learning are essential for the professional seafarer, whether mooring master, deck personnel, bridge operator, or vessel traffic controller. From the standpoint of the industry, we're zeroing in on *excellence*. We want to see professionalism enhanced and help to protect the marine environment. We must be ahead of the game at all times, not responding to yesterday's needs."

Larsson stresses good bridge and wheelhouse management practices. "When an accident occurs," he says, "it is usually the result of a failure to keep a proper lookout, or a breakdown in good bridge or wheelhouse management practices. Good bridge management efficiently uses all of the available resources of manpower and equipment, ensuring there is a systematic bridge organization which will get a ship safely from one port to another. We incorporate bridge team training and coordination into all of our professional education courses," Larsson explains.[160]

A graduate of the U.S. Merchant Marine Academy, Larsson earned a master's degree in education at Fordham University, where he is now a doctoral candidate. He also holds a chief mate license, having sailed for seven years on tankers and cargo ships.

Below left to right: Captain Richard K. Beadon, Eric K. Larsson, and James J. Fitzpatrick III

Several organizations, among them SCI, responded immediately to the plight of the immigrants and seafarers. Stevenson set out at once to put the center's considerable experience in maritime law at the disposal of the defense counsel representing the crew. The court-appointed lawyers were, in Stevenson's estimation, "strong advocates," but they were not familiar with the maritime industry or maritime crewing practices. Stevenson visited the arrested ship, advised defense counsel at court hearings, and helped the lawyers coordinate their defense and prepare for trial. Utilizing the Institute's international contacts, SCI staffers obtained information vital to the crew's defense from port chaplains in Taiwan, Kenya, Thailand, Singapore, and Hong Kong. Meanwhile, the Reverend Jean R. Smith, director of SCI's Center for Seafarers' Services and of the Institute's International Seafarers' Center in Port Newark/Port Elizabeth,

World War II veteran status for U.S. merchant mariners. The Institute helped lead the fight for the rights of seafarers who served in the U.S. merchant marine. In January 1988, the Defense Department announced that World War II veteran status had been awarded to merchant seafarers who sailed during the period of armed conflict in World War II.

briefed officials at the Indonesian Consulate on the plight of the *Golden Venture* crew. Next she lined up a Burmese-speaking chaplain and an Indonesian-speaking chaplain to accompany her on visits to the crew members in prison, once permission for visits was obtained from the authorities. "We don't know how many of the crew will want to have a pastoral visit," Smith said at the time, "and we're not making any assumptions. We're simply ready. We have two chaplains ready to receive a telephone call and to drop everything to go."

Eventually most of the crew members pleaded guilty to a lesser offense than originally charged, and as this book went to press, they were about to be turned over to Immigration for repatriation. Stevenson expected next to provide the defense counsel with referrals for the seafarers for Immigration lawyers to assist them in their repatriation. "I can think of no case that better exemplifies what we are doing here," he said. "It all comes down to the basic premise that we are here to be friends of the friendless. The crew of the *Golden Venture* needed our help. And, like anyone who has a friend in trouble, we offer whatever assistance that we can."

The Reverend Dr. James R. Whittemore put his finger on the major challenge facing maritime chaplains: "West meets East," SCI's then-director pronounced at an International Christian Maritime Association (ICMA) conference in the Philippines. "The overwhelming majority of seafarers today are from Asian countries, yet the chaplains in most ports are mainly English-speaking westerners. We need more chaplains who represent the cross-cultural populations they serve."[161]

At the Institute's International Seafarers' Center in Port Newark/Port Elizabeth, the already skilled port chaplains and multilingual ship visitors were retrained to recognize and deal quickly with shipboard problems occasioned by language and cultural differences as well as increased stress at sea. New staff members were hired who could speak not only Spanish and Greek, but also Hindi, Japanese, Malayalam, Mandarin, Korean, and Tagalog. On a larger scale, to further bridge the cross-cultural gap between the ever-increasing Asian work force and the chaplains who ministered in North American ports, the Institute in 1987, with the help of the Henry Luce Foundation, established the Asian/North American Pastoral Training Program. Since then, the Institute has appointed several Asian/North American Fellows each year, and with the Port of New York and New Jersey as their laboratory, seasoned pastors experienced in Asian culture and language have come to train at the International Seafarers' Center from the Philippines, Korea, Burma, Singapore, and Malaysia.

In many ways, the International Seafarers' Center in the 1970s and 1980s offered what SCI had always offered, as one visitor noted: "Upstairs is a small chapel for nightly services. Down a set of stairs and through a passageway is a small bar where men sip beer — the Nicene Creed and good grog, salvation and a watering hole secure from the vultures ashore."[162] SCI ship visitors met two-thirds of all ships arriving in port, their arms full of *National Geographic* magazines, subway maps, Bibles in Tagalog, or whatever else might interest a crew of diverse international origins. Yet the modern Institute offered other help as well. "We have a two-pronged goal," the Reverend Barbara C. Crafton, then director of the Seafarers' Services Division, succinctly stated in early 1986. "One is restoring human spirits, often badly damaged by dehumanizing shipboard work. Second is the defense of seamen's rights. Often seafarers aren't aware of already existing legal protections that are part of their vessel's registry. We listen to their problems, give them practical guidance, and frequently intercede with authorities to attempt to correct an injustice."[163] After the Center for Seafarers' Rights was established in 1982, chaplains were encouraged to call upon the center for advice, and by the end of the decade they were working hand-in-hand with the center's attorneys.

Changes in the nature of seafarers' work made the chaplains' services even more important in the 1970s and 1980s than in the past. "In former years, maritime work was dangerous and lonely, involving intense alienation from normal life on land," Crafton continued. "But it wasn't particularly stressful since seamen had plenty of time on board to pursue personal interests and a lot of time in ports to see what often were romantic or exotic places." On modern ships, however, that has all changed. With smaller crews, everyone is indispensable. Perpetual routines of four hours on and four hours off, plus very short turnaround times in port, have created severe stress-related health problems. "Add to this the alienation endemic in doing a repetitive mechanical job, and the knowledge that there are far more seafarers who want to work than there are positions in the industry, and you have a work force with what can best be described as a siege mentality."[164]

By 1988, there were an estimated 10,000 to 12,000 retired or unemployed seafarers in the New York metropolitan area, and a senior chaplain at the Institute estimated that SCI chaplains were conducting nearly 1,500 interviews and counseling sessions a year, with both active seafarers and those on the beach.

By the summer of 1990, when the Reverend Jean Smith became director of the Seafarers' Services Division as well as the International Seafarers' Center, and brought her considerable pastoral and organizational skills to the Institute,

Alfred Lee Loomis, III

"The safety-at-sea emphasis is what I want to make sure comes across," said Chip Loomis, chairman of SCI's board of managers, when asked about the Institute's mission in the 1990s.

One of those rare individuals who grasps both the "big picture" and the nitty-gritty details, Loomis was elected chairman of SCI's board of managers in 1992 after twenty years of service on the board, seven as president. During these years he was instrumental in revamping the financial structure of the Institute under Whittemore and was a strong and effective leader in securing board support for building the new headquarters at Water Street. Working with board members Anthony D. Marshall and George D. Benjamin, chairman of the nominating committee, he helped forge an effective, dedicated board whose members were largely recruited from the shipping industry, maritime labor organizations, and New York City institutions.

Passionate on the topic of safety, Loomis was also a key player in redirecting SCI's mission away from "bedrooms" to its current focus on safety-at-sea through maritime education and seafarers' rights. "Everything the Institute does focuses on seafarers — their physical training in terms of duties and shipboard life," Loomis elaborates. "Everything from booklets on AIDS, alcohol counseling, lending the seafarer money while in port, legal counseling — so when the ship goes to sea the seafarer is better prepared emotionally, spiritually, physically, and better trained. So it's more likely that the seas will be safe. And the environment will be, as a corollary thereof, better protected."

Loomis sees the chairman's role as one of directing the Institute toward its mission and making important strategic-planning decisions. One goal in particular is to see all the nations of the world "pulling together" under the same safety and training standards. The institute, Loomis feels, can be a real influence for change to improve laws, international standards, and business practices that affect the lives of seafarers.

Loomis is a general partner of the Downtown Associates and serves on the Fales committee of the U.S. Naval Academy and on the board of Mystic Seaport. He is also vice-commodore of the New York Yacht Club.

Below left to right: Henry C. B. Lindh, the Reverend Dr. James R. Whittemore, the Reverend Peter Larom, Alfred Loomis III

AIDS Booklets

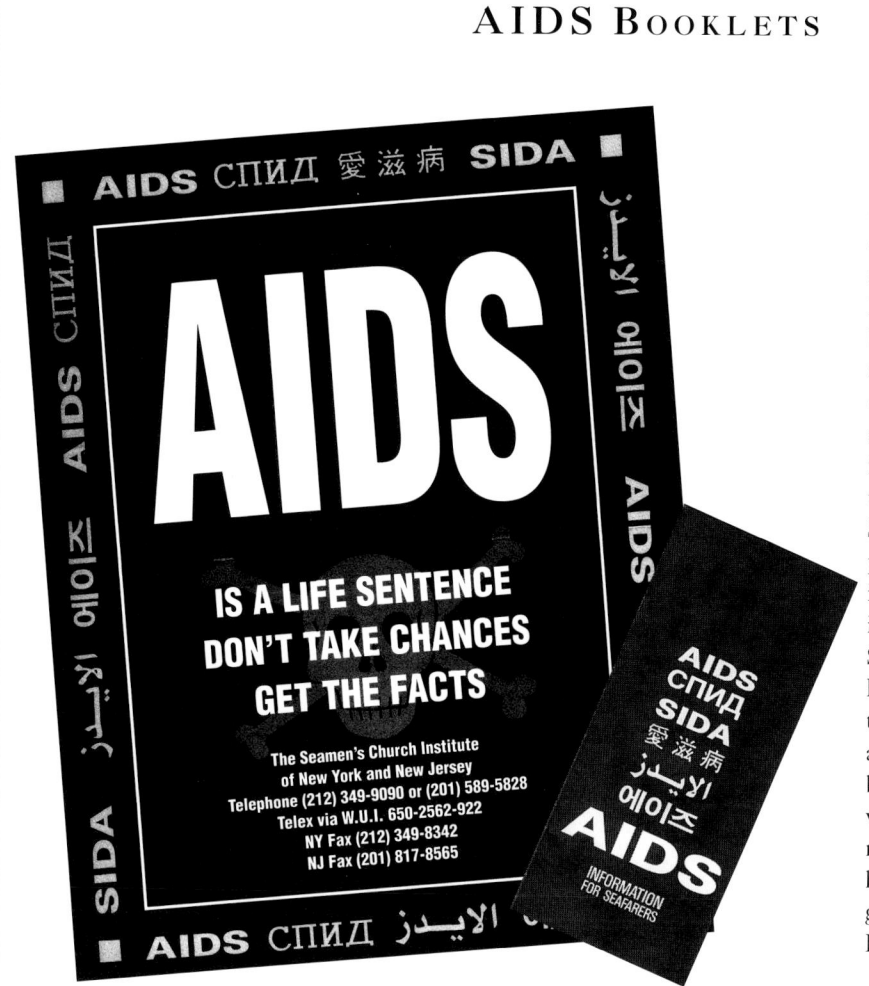

In the late 1980s, the Danish Directorate for Seafarers published a short pamphlet containing specific, concrete facts about HIV infection and AIDS. The Seamen's Church Institute, which for some time had been concerned about the special risk seafarers ran of contracting the disease, chose the Danish pamphlet as the best treatment of the subject for seafarers. With the permission of the Danish Directorate for Seafarers, SCI prepared and expanded the pamphlet — originally published in Danish and English — and translated it into Chinese, Korean, Greek, and Spanish. Available at the Institute's Port Newark and New York centers, the pamphlet is also distributed aboard ship by SCI ship visitors and by ICMA chaplains throughout the world. As this book went to press, more than 100,000 AIDS booklets had been distributed in eight languages, the most recent of which was Indonesian.

---

the ship visiting staff had expanded to eight. In addition to the core group of pastors, there were volunteer ship visitors, seminarians who came as summer interns, and the Asian chaplains funded by the Luce Foundation. The Asian/North American Pastoral Training Program had become extremely successful in preparing clergy and lay people to minister to seafarers and manage seafarers' centers in North America and East Asia, and in the summer of 1992, it was expanded and renamed the International Training Center for Maritime Ministry (ITC). An umbrella for the chaplain training programs offered by the Institute, ITC encompassed an intensive ten-month internship for experienced clergy, a ten-week summer intern program for seminarians and clergy in maritime ministry, and a flexible program for clergy in the New York City area interested in the maritime workplace experience. Topics included ministering to a multicultural population, dealing with seafarers' rights issues, and approaching maritime ministry from an ecumenical perspective.[165]

The exotic mix of individuals and the complexities of the chaplain-seafarer and chaplain-chaplain relationships that Smith confronts in the daily course of her work often make for heady discussion. "Let me speak from a different

The Reverend Peter Larom

"One can't be around Peter and not want to be a part of what he is addressing; his enthusiasm is infectious," offered a former colleague of Peter Larom.

From the day he replaced retiring director Jim Whittemore on October 1, 1992, Larom's energy, tenacity, and vision have impressed SCI's board members, staff, volunteers, and friends. "Peter doesn't walk, he flies," observed one staff member. The new director seems everywhere, involved in everything. On any given day, he can be found facilitating a roundtable discussion, welcoming dignitaries from the international maritime community, or in the Seafarers' Club making sandwiches and serving lunch to seafarers. He has been seen moving ship-model cases, directing photo shoots, cajoling local vendors to contribute to a special event — all seemingly at the same time.

In the short time Larom has been at the Institute, he has immersed himself in the maritime community, meeting with players from industry, government, the port, and the media, and he has strengthened relationships with the lower Manhattan community and SCI's neighbors. Under his direction, the Water Street Galleries have become a reality, and the Institute was able to welcome home from storage many of the ship models from its private collection.[166]

No stranger to the maritime world, Larom worked two summers as a seafarer while in high school, beginning as a deck boy on the MT *Margaret Onstad*, the SS *Troll*, and the MT *Olympic Valley*. "I swabbed decks and hauled cartons," he recently recalled. "I was the lowest of the low."[167] Nonetheless, he cherishes his seafaring memories and keeps his old *Avregningsbok* (ship card) on his desk.

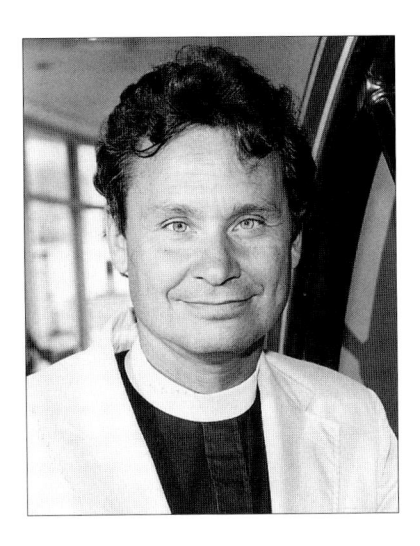

Larom's career has run the gamut from local community concerns to international affairs. After graduating from Cornell University and General Theological Seminary, he was named rector of a troubled church in Astoria, Queens. In a short time, he built the parish and founded a community development corporation to revitalize the neighborhood. Next came a stint in Uganda, where he and his wife taught at a seminary, then a relief mission to the Sudan, which at the time was ravaged by severe drought. Larom's skills in dealing with officials came to the fore when he commandeered three Libyan Air Force jets to take food and medical supplies into the desert. "If your cause is good, people will usually respond," he said at the time."[168]

Upon returning to the United States, Larom and his family joined the Grace Church community in White Plains, New York, where, the *New York Times* reported, he became a "local legend" for his advocacy of the homeless and the hungry, those addicted to drugs and alcohol, and others in need of help here and throughout the county.[169]

A man with a kaleidoscopic eye, Larom sees several important areas of need when he considers SCI's mission. "One is protection," he says. "Protection of the maritime environment, protection of the lives of seafarers and passengers aboard ships, and protection of jobs." Second, in an industry that has become mechanized and intermodal and has caused a shrinking job market, SCI needs to minister to seafarers who want to make job changes or need help in retirement. "There are ratings who are out there in the cold who need housing, job referrals, career retreading, and hand-holding," Larom points out. Third, while Larom reiterates the Institute's important links to industry and its successful example of ministry to the workplace, he wants to dust off SCI's links to its church base. "To do ministry doesn't mean ministry only to Christians," he says. "Our thrust is interfaith. But our motivation and call is church based, and we want to re-cement our historical ties, not just to the Episcopal Church but to downtown churches in our community as well."

---

perspective than the cold, hard details," Smith suggested to a recent visitor at the International Seafarers' Center. "Let's say a seafarer from a Third-World country has been arrested for allegedly smuggling drugs. We have a chaplain of that nationality, and he goes to the ship and gets the story — whatever the story is." Perhaps the story is that the seafarer was asked to deliver a box, but insists he did not know its contents. How does the chaplain respond?

First, Smith says, the chaplain may be outraged that his countryman has been innocently dragged into a criminal action. But he also knows that smuggling is a way of life in his country, "and of course there's a chance the seafarer knows *exactly* what he's doing. Then the chaplain may feel ashamed of his countrymen, feeling momentarily that his people are unsophisticated, or stupid, or thieves.

"Now," says Smith, "How are we going to care for this chaplain? How are we going to listen and take our cues from him in terms of what kind of care is appropriate — what does he need today?" No matter how much theological education the pastors have had, no matter how much training in parish work, the daily life at the Seamen's Church Institute presents an ever-changing challenge.

To overcome these trials, Smith envisions a revolving ministry of short-term stays by port pastors and visitors from throughout the world. "We are reorganizing and refocusing the training program to meet the needs of this decade of seafarers," she notes. "Training port chaplains in the humanitarian rights of seafarers is part of our pastoral call and special knowledge required to meet spiritual needs."[170]

Since its inception, the Institute has been committed to improving safety at sea, and since the days of Captain Robert Huntington during World War I has provided comprehensive maritime training for merchant seafarers. During the 1970s and 1980s, technological advances in shipping, new licensing and certification requirements in the industry — and changes in the way steamship companies viewed the education of their employees — forced the Institute constantly to fine-tune its programs. "There used to be little training inside the companies," SCI deputy director Frank Huntington (no relation to Robert Huntington) said in an interview in 1985. "They relegated the training to the unions and the unions in turn relegated training to the Coast Guard. Now interest in training is returning to the companies." Several private companies, as well as the Coast Guard, have asked the Institute to design special training programs for their employees.[171]

A particular strength of the Institute has been the training of officers and seafarers in radar and advanced radar techniques. In the fall of 1985, the first radar training conference ever to be held in the United States took place at the Institute. Representatives from sixteen of eighteen radar training schools for merchant seafarers gathered at SCI to meet with U.S. government officials, Coast Guard representatives, and delegates from foreign nations to discuss the standardization and upgrading of basic radar training and recertification methods.[172] Unlike the European nations at the time, the United States did not require formal training in the use of automatic radar plotting aids, even though all vessels of 10,000 gross tons or more calling at U.S. ports and carrying hazardous cargo in bulk were required to be fitted with ARPA units. The delegation at the conference drafted resolutions directed toward voluntarily setting U.S. stan-

> ### THE HONORABLE ANTHONY D. MARSHALL
>
> Following in the footsteps of his stepfather, Charles H. Marshall, Tony Marshall joined the board in 1963. He was soon posted abroad as American ambassador to various locales, including the Malagasy Republic, Trinidad and Tobago, Kenya, and the Seychelles, but he maintained close ties to the Institute, and when he retired from diplomatic service, he followed John Winslow in 1980 as president of the board of managers.
>
> "He came to the job with diplomatic skills and social standing," a former SCI staffer recalled, "and he basically dealt with the Institute in the same perceptive and diplomatic way" he had dealt with his various embassies. Through his many connections and those of his mother, Brooke Astor, Marshall broadened the Institute's base of support and lent a solid financial hand during its fiscal troubles in the 1980s.

dards of simulator training equivalent to those set by the International Maritime Organization in 1978.[173]

By the early 1970s, SCI's radar training program was using special simulator equipment that realistically duplicated typical navigational situations encountered by merchant watchkeepers. Technological advances were so rapid, however, that by the mid-1980s it was clear to the board that even more sophisticated equipment was necessary. In 1984, a special advisory committee sent Eric K. Larsson, director of SCI's Center for Maritime Education, on a two-year search for the best maritime training simulator available. After much deliberation, the board chose the state-of-the-art simulator made by Norcontrol of Norway. The Norcontrol simulator was installed at SCI in 1987, with great pride and fanfare.

Also known as T-GIS (Transputer-Generated Imaging System), the simulator was the first of its kind in the United States, and it could provide crews with ship-handling experience that typically took years to acquire through conventional methods. Four SCI classrooms were converted into four ships' bridges that operated independently or in concert. The video and audio simulation is so realistic that a first-time experience can be stunning. One reporter who was given an introduction to the simulator called it "New York's most expensive electronic game: video tanker." She offered this vivid description of a simulated voyage:

> It is a black night, with no moon. I guide my 700-foot oil tanker past Ambrose Light and into New York Harbor. Lighted buoys mark my way. Other lights flicker around me. I'm confused. Suddenly, through the windows of the bridge, I see a hulking, portentous shape, darker even than the night. I swing the helm hard to starboard. My giant vessel doesn't budge. The tanker's bow is on my bridge.
>
> "I think we can safely say that you've crashed into another oil tanker," says my chief mate, stationed at my elbow.[174]

JOHN G. WINSLOW

Elected president of the board of managers to succeed Franklin Vilas when he retired December 31, 1969, John Winslow had been a board member since 1959. He had full confidence that the Institute could and would survive, he once said, but only with effective and conservative managers who really understood SCI's underlying structure. A warm and charming man, he worked quietly but effectively behind the scenes and contributed greatly to the board by carefully ferreting out talented individuals to serve SCI with skill and devotion. He was also instrumental in the establishment of the Development Office.

"Video tanker," however, was no game. As tankers became larger and larger and carried greater cargoes of oil, the potential for environmental disaster grew proportionally, a lesson taught all too painfully by the *Exxon Valdez* incident in Alaska. Regular, comprehensive training helped prevent the accidents at sea that cost billions of dollars in loss of life, cargo, and equipment, and in environmental damage — a point driven home to the reporter who "crashed" on the simulator. "The only reason no oil spilled and I wasn't being hauled up on charges," she ruefully observed, "is that I was stationed at the Seamen's Church Institute" and not at the helm of a real tanker.[175]

For the seafarers, explained Larsson, "a lot of the training is 'what if.'" By tapping on a computer keyboard, Larsson can produce what-if situations worthy of the caprice of Father Neptune himself on a particularly cranky day. An unaware trainee serenely scanning the horizon might suddenly be blinded by a rain squall, find the navigation system knocked out or the engine cut, discover the wind backing and increasing to hurricane force — and, at the same time, be required to respond to the panicked screech of a small-craft captain's "MAYDAY! MAYDAY!" coming over the VHF radio. In Larsson's estimation, "When you're out on the water, you might experience years without a problem. But then comes the time that something happens that's different. That's where much of the value in the training comes in."[176]

Even the exalted Norcontrol equipment needed routine updating, and in 1992 the simulator's training field was expanded to five screens; these encompassed a 200° horizontal field of view for the trainee positioned at the simulated bridge, with a vertical field of 30°. At a preview, SCI office workers crowded into the new five-screen bridge to watch the "captain" steer up New York Harbor. As Larsson took the simulator through its paces at dawn, daytime, dusk, and night, and demonstrated the many types of harbor craft that could be made to move through the waters — among the red and green buoys bowing in the wake

115

Henry C. B. Lindh

A member of the board of managers since 1961, Harry Lindh for more than thirty years has overseen the sometimes tortured finances of the Institute, first as treasurer and now as president of the board.

Lindh recalls with amusement the days when only the president of the board and SCI's director were allowed to see the Institute's financial statements — a policy Lindh immediately lobbied to change when he was elected treasurer in 1966. "What I've tried to do over this period is update the Institute's financial and accounting records into the current era," he says with characteristic enthusiasm. "I provide financial information to the board to allow them to make better business decisions."

In 1992, the grateful board elected Lindh its president. Often described by his colleagues as someone who cuts through all the nonsense, gets down to basics, and presses for decisions, Lindh now oversees the nuts-and-bolts of the day-to-day running of the Institute. He is, as one staffer recently said, "the person people ultimately look to when it comes to spending money."

---

of passing ships — the vista seemed so real to one of the office workers that she left the room, saying, "I can't watch it. I get seasick."[177]

In 1990, Mobil Marine Transportation selected SCI's Center for Maritime Education to provide simulator training for its inland tug and barge fleet. "Maintaining the highest level of professional skills of our U.S. fleet personnel is a cornerstone of our concern for safety," said Gerhard E. Kurz, general manager of Mobil Oil Marine Corporation's Worldwide Marine Transportation and president of Mobil Shipping and Transportation Company — and member of SCI's board of managers. "SCI's enhanced program will provide a sophisticated tool that will help them carry out their important mission."[178]

As this book went to press, the Center for Maritime Education was raising funds to set up a Global Maritime Distress and Safety System (GMDSS) regional command station at its training center. Designed to aid in the identification and coordination of search-and-rescue efforts of all vessels on the high seas, the GMDSS could eliminate the possibility of ships disappearing without a trace. The system, which embraces satellites and transistor-based electronics, enables ship-to-shore, shore-to-ship, and ship-to-ship communication within four areas of the world's oceans. Digital selective calling provides information about the ship transmitting the call: an identification number, the nature of the distress, and the time and coordinates of the distress. This information is broadcast automatically to all ships on a variety of frequencies in many bands to increase the possibility that the message will be heard. Far more effective than the current combination of radiotelepathy and Morse code, "GMDSS," says Alfred Lee Loomis III, chairman of SCI's board, "makes the 'Sparks' radio operator a thing of the past."

According to parameters set by the International Maritime Organization, ninety-seven percent of the world's merchant fleet will be required to operate

GMDSS by 1999; eventually, fishing, recreational, and small passenger ships may also need to comply. Over the next several years, at least 250,000 ships' officers will need training. Spurred by grants from the Life Saving Benevolent Association, the Henry L. and Grace Doherty Foundation, and Kloster Cruise Lines, SCI's Center for Maritime Education recently began offering a GMDSS training course.

Indeed, the Center for Maritime Education has been at the cutting edge of maritime education and training programs since its inception. It has specialized in designing courses and training programs to assist the shipping industry when new rules and regulations developed regarding the introduction of new maritime equipment and procedures. The center has thus enhanced the individual seafarer's professional competency and promoted safety of life at sea.

That SCI's Center for Seafarers' Rights, and its maritime education and social services programs functioned so well and so smoothly by the early 1990s owed a great deal to the highly capable leadership of the board of managers and to the Reverend Dr. James R. Whittemore, who in 1977 took the helm as SCI's new director.

Whittemore came at a time of bleak financial outlook for the Institute. Increasing operating costs and the industry-wide depression in shipping had sent the deficit soaring. Bookings at SCI's hotel were off. American seafarers worked the new intermodal containerships, which were rarely in port long enough for a sailor to need a hotel room. Most of the old "tramps" were worked by Third-World seafarers who could not afford to stay at the Institute, even with its low rates. Thus, the new State Street building was not breaking even, and the hotel was draining the Institute. Faced with these problems, the board sought and found in Whittemore an aggressive and forward-looking individual to assess the situation and face it head-on.

At his formal installation on April 7, 1977, Whittemore laid out the facts to more than two hundred assembled guests and friends of the Institute. Over the last nine years, he told them, the endowment had been spent down to offset deficits and pay for the building at 15 State Street. Taking the present deficit into consideration, the Institute could expect to carry on for about another five years. "The probability, however, of celebrating our 150th anniversary in 1984 is rather dim, unless there is a radical reversal of our economic fortunes. I tell you all this," Whittemore informed his audience, "to correct the general notion that we are a heavily endowed organization with no financial problems. This is just not the case."[179] He later wrote, "Secretly within myself, I wondered if the Institute had outworn its usefulness; whether, indeed, my task was to orchestrate the orderly dissolution of the world's largest and most honored seafarer's society."[180]

As previous SCI directors had done when taking over, Whittemore asked the board to engage a management planning consultant to evaluate SCI's operation. The firm of Robert C. Sorenson and Associates was hired and in due time submitted an astute and detailed evaluation. Sorenson concluded that SCI's most important operation was its ship visiting program. "Yet," he pointed out, "less time, money and effort are given to ship visiting than to any other major SCI operation." Sorenson acknowledged that the hotel was a useful service to seafarers, but he also saw quite clearly that "it must be run on an effective business basis regardless of the charitable role in which we have cast ourselves." The food-and-beverage operation, open to the public as well as to seafarers, had caused a serious financial drain. Overall, Sorenson recommended a sweeping overhaul of SCI's operations.

The board immediately took Sorenson's recommendations to heart, and over the next four years, it authorized significant administrative changes and aggressive fund-raising strategies. By 1980, aided by a major challenge grant of $1,000,000 from the Astor Foundation, the Institute was close to having a balanced budget. The ship visiting program was strengthened. A new emphasis on safety at sea at SCI's Merchant Marine School, and the teaching of the Rules of the Road to Coast Guard personnel and others, enabled the Institute to take over the federal government's largest radar training facility in 1982.

Despite this solid progress in focusing the work of the Institute and bringing its deficit budget within manageable size, a financial crisis of major proportions occurred in the middle of 1981. By now the Institute's hotel — its primary source

Mobil advertorial. Maritime training at the Seamen's Church Institute has always been held in high esteem within the shipping industry. After the *Exxon Valdez* catastrophe, Mobil took out advertisements in various publications. This one appeared in the *New York Times* and in *Time* magazine.

Sea saga

Dawn breaks over New York harbor. A young captain-in-training at the helm of a 5,000-horsepower tugboat pushes a 400-foot barge through the rising mist. Under the seasoned guidance of a senior captain, he heads toward the Hudson River and upstate New York with five million gallons of home-heating oil. Just off the starboard bow, he can faintly make out the Staten Island ferry, and it's clearly on a steady bearing. That means it's on a collision course. He asks the senior captain: "What do you want to do?" But the senior captain doesn't answer; he's just had a heart attack and died.

This melodrama will never earn an Oscar or a Tony, but it's just the kind of saga a would-be captain might find himself starring in at The Seamen's Church Institute (SCI) in New York City—a charitable organization with a long and proud history of onshore aid to mariners from all over the world.

SCI operates a renowned maritime training school—one of a handful using "visual ship-simulators" in the classroom to create navigation scenarios. From the windows of a mock ship's bridge, a trainee can view a computer-generated image of a real-life harbor or waterway with moving marine traffic—including ships piloted by fellow trainees. The scene might be day or night, dusk or dawn, blue skies or Hurricane Bob. And as the trainee "moves" the vessel, so moves the image that is seen.

Ship-simulation would be the ultimate video game if it weren't such serious business. It puts a trainee in the driver's seat at no risk to people, ships, cargoes or water. That's one of the reasons Mobil and other ship operators send marine personnel to SCI for training. And that's why Mobil recently made a donation to prime the pump of SCI's million-dollar Simulator Enhancement Program—a campaign to make the training even more technologically realistic and effective than it is now.

Mobil shares SCI's mission to promote safety and environmental protection at sea. We're among the oil industry's leaders in the development of oil-spill response and training programs. And soon our capabilities will be backed up by the Marine Spill Response Corporation, an industry partnership we helped create last year to combat spills in the U.S. Yet we fervently believe prevention is the best medicine, as the saying goes. So we developed a patented double-bottom crude-oil tanker in the 1960s, and we recently commissioned a double-hull tanker with a second steel skin enveloping most of the vessel. We also exhaustively inspect our own ships and the ships we contract to make sure they're sound. And now we're helping busy commercial ports upgrade their navigation management systems.

Strong ships and systems alone won't protect the environment. Ultimately, safety depends upon people. And no one is more interested in our precious marine environment than the men and women who choose to spend their working lives there.

So we promote safety through the stringent training of our personnel and through superior organizations like SCI—one of the best shipmates a ship operator could ask for. To find out how you can help fund the Simulator Enhancement Program, write to Rev. James R. Whittemore, Director, The Seamen's Church Institute, 241 Water Street, New York, New York 10038.

Mobil

© 1991 Mobil Corporation

Charles E. Saltzman. In a brief ecumenical service prior to the 1993 annual meeting of the board of managers, Charles E. Saltzman, a limited partner of Goldman Sachs & Co., was awarded a silver bell in honor of his sixty years of volunteer service to the Institute, the longest period anyone had served as a member of the Institute's board.

of income — was operating at only sixty percent of occupancy rather than at the projected seventy-five percent. Unexpected energy cost increases were $150,000 above budget, and the city began to assess the Institute $40,000 to $50,000 a year for sewage and water charges. The projected deficit for 1981 soared from about $250,000 to $750,000. Compounding these financial difficulties was the discovery that SCI's capital funds in terms of unrestricted legacies were almost exhausted.

First among several changes was a revision of the Institute's Statement of Purpose and Mission. For nearly 150 years, SCI had been operating under an outdated act of incorporation that stated that "the object of the Seamen's Church Institute . . . is to provide . . . floating and other churches for Seamen in the city and port of New York . . . in which churches, the seats shall be free; and to provide suitable clergymen to act as Missionaries in said churches." In October 1982, a Revised Statement of Purpose was unanimously approved:

> Recognizing that international trade is essential to the welfare of the global community, the Seamen's Church Institute of New York and New Jersey is dedicated to the safety, well-being, dignity, and professional competence of seafarers and those who work in international transportation and commerce, and affirms its obligation to strengthen through its programs the essential link between religious and secular values within society.

But the greatest changes came in June 1982, when the board reached its most momentous decision: that SCI should discontinue providing hotel accommodations and a public food service at its Manhattan headquarters building. On November 10, 1983, the board agreed to sell the State Street building. After consultations with many individuals, including SCI board members Richard S. Berry and William Whiting, who were real estate professionals, and Ralph K. Smith, Jr., the Institute's attorney, the board in 1984 entertained bids for the sale of 15 State Street. As the Institute celebrated 150 years of service to seafarers in January 1985 with a gala maritime ball and benefit dinner held aboard the *Intrepid* at Pier 86 in Manhattan, Berry and Smith completed arduous negotia-

CHRISTMAS-AT-SEA

Augusta de Peyster, second from left

In 1898, during the Spanish-American War, a certain Mrs. E.A. Gardner conceived the idea of supplying "our" warships with "just what they needed," the Reverend Walter A.A. Gardner, chaplain of the North River Station, noted in his Annual Report. "Noble-hearted friends came to her assistance. The *New York Herald* and the Associated Press took it up, and thousands of [comfort] bags, medical supplies, delicacies, Bible prayerbooks, testaments, and many cases of literature were sent to our men; and as one of the results, letters are written and received from our seamen from all parts of the world."[181] Thus began an SCI tradition of supplying ditty bags to sailors during wartime and to shipwrecked crews. From ditty bags to woolen goods for "our" sailors at Christmas time was but a small leap of inspiration, and out of this work eventually grew the Christmas-at-Sea program.

At the turn of the century, Augusta M. de Peyster organized a handful of friends and founded the Seamen's Benefit Society as a ladies' auxiliary to SCI. The society quickly became an important fund-raising arm of the Institute, collecting money for tea and theater parties, picnics, and reading materials, and providing knitted articles and ditty bags for the British apprentice lads and other seafarers stopping by the Institute. During World War I, this work expanded, particularly through the distribution of knitted articles and ditty bags. By World War II, women throughout the United States were knitting garments for merchant seafarers, and thousands of sweaters, socks, "helmets," mufflers, and mittens filled the Institute's Sloppe Chest. But the wartime need was acute, and even more knitted articles were needed. Someone got the idea of providing free wool to the knitters, and the knitting program took off — particu-

tions with JMB Realty of Chicago, and the closing was set for March 1985.

The sale of the building — for more than $29 million — strengthened the endowment and allowed the Institute to press on with its work.

Whittemore believed that the Institute's history and current activities had now come full circle. "We originally got into the business of housing seafarers in response to the exploitation they were suffering at the hands of the crimps and

Patricia Jones (second from right), director of the Christmas-at-Sea program working with some of her volunteers and the Reverend Jean R. Smith (far right)

larly after Pearl Harbor, when the increased patriotic fervor brought many new friends offering their services as volunteers, eager to "do their bit" for the brave men of the merchant marine. In 1942, there were about 2,000 "good friends" knitting, sewing, and filling Christmas boxes at the Institute, aided by other organizations and groups, including about sixty women's auxiliaries of churches of all denominations throughout the United States. That year, about 5,000 boxes were distributed by SCI ship visitors to the crews of freighters and tankers in New York Harbor who spent Christmas Day on the high seas. Every seafarer who spent Christmas Eve at 25 South Street — with accommodations for 1,600 — also received a box.

What began as a hurry-up war effort today is a national volunteer program, involving more than 3,000 knitters from every state in the nation. Some knitters are part of church groups; others are independent. Each year some 6,000 scarves, 3,000 sweaters, and 1,000 pairs of socks — 16,000 knitted garments all told — pour into the Institute. Throughout the year, other volunteers, some 300 strong, gather at the Institute to pack these and other useful items (stationery kits, combs, atlases, etc.) into Christmas-at-Sea boxes. Each box includes a homemade, handwritten greeting card that carries love and cheer to merchant seafarers who sail into the Port of New York and New Jersey.

Today the program is coordinated by Pat Jones, widow of Coast Guard Commander Glenn D. Jones. She "walked into" the Christmas room at the Institute in 1975 "to see if I could help in some way"— and has been there ever since.

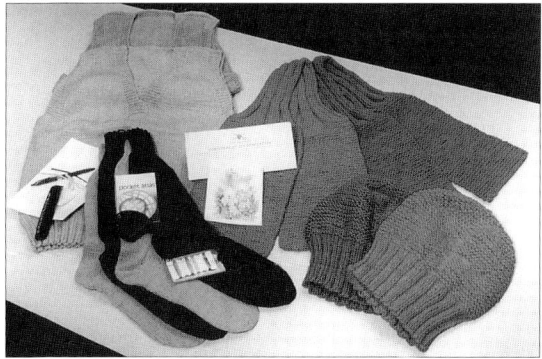

Inside a Christmas-at-Sea package a seafarer may find a handknit sweater vest, stationery, and a sewing kit, among other useful items.

boardinghouse operators in the late 19th and early 20th centuries," he said. "Now, the exploitation of seafarers takes a different form — not housing ashore, but conditions aboard certain ships." By moving out of the housing business and concentrating SCI's efforts into programs like the Center for Seafarers' Rights, the Institute would once again be able to focus its concern where seafarers needed it most. "So," Whittemore concluded, "as we did under Dr. Mansfield's leadership many years ago, we are changing our physical surroundings in order to better fulfill our mission of service to seafarers."[182]

In March 1985, the Institute weighed anchor and moved from its home for the previous seventeen years to a temporary billet, taking up new quarters in rented space in an office building at 50 Broadway. After a three-year search to secure a waterfront location, Whittemore and the board chose a site for a new headquarters building at 237-243 Water Street, in the South Street Seaport Historic District in lower Manhattan. SCI was returning to its roots. The new site was midway between the old 25 South Street location and Pike's Slip, where in 1844 SCI had launched its mission with the first Floating Church of Our Saviour. Furthermore, it included the 190-year-old Schermerhorn, Banker & Co. Ship Chandlery, once operated by the family of Peter Augustus Schermerhorn, a founding patron and board member of the fledgling Protestant Episcopal Church Missionary Society for Seamen. In these new-but-old surroundings, as Whittemore pointed out, SCI could perpetuate its historic mission and "inter-relate in a very real way with the Seaport."[183] With funds raised by Niels W. Johnsen, chairman of the board's development committee, the Institute in 1988 purchased the site for $3.2 million.

During the Institute's time at 50 Broadway, SCI seemed so anonymous that some people thought it had gone out of business. For this reason, Richard Berry, now chairman of the board's building committee, felt it was important that the Institute "have a symbol" in the new headquarters building. To make its presence known again, SCI planned a striking something-old-something-new structure incorporating the facade of the ship chandlery, rather than a design that would simply blend inconspicuously with Water Street's early 19th-century ambiance. The architectural firm of James Stewart Polshek and Partners, with Mr. Polshek and Richard Olcott as principal designers, achieved a stunning design with nautical overtones that represented a symbolic blend of the world into which SCI was born and the world in which it now lives. Groundbreaking for the $12 million building took place in July 1989, and in May 1991 the official opening of the new Seamen's Church Institute was celebrated at a joyful "Dedication of Service." Actress Brooke Shields smashed a traditional bottle of Moët & Chandon champagne over the entrance as ships' bells rang out on vessels in the East River and hundreds of guests blew boatswain's whistles. More than a dozen religious leaders — Christian, Hindu, Muslim and Jewish — participated, and ten port chaplains serving the New York and New Jersey area recited Psalm 65 in English, Tagalog, Mandarin, Korean, French, German, and Spanish.

The meshing of old and new underscored the continuing, if changed, role

The *Titanic* Memorial where it stands today at Fulton and Water Streets

of the Institute in New York's seafaring life. The new headquarters reflected the board's refocusing of its priorities; there are no hotel accommodations, but ample space is allocated to the Center for Seafarers' Rights and the Center for Maritime Education. Sharing the premises are a comfortable and homey Seafarers' Club, with snack bar, reading room, and counseling office, and a bright, airy room for the Christmas-at-Sea program. On the ground floor, the modern but intimate chapel showcases the original baptismal font from the first Floating Church of Our Saviour.

A year after the new building's dedication, in his final Annual Report before retirement, Whittemore spoke gratefully of his "opportunity to serve this distinguished organization" and summarized the many "sea changes" that had beset the Institute and the maritime industry since he assumed SCI's directorship in 1977. For mariners, Whittemore explained, "Sea changes are bewildering times when weather shifts radically, the patterns of the tides reverse, the wind shifts and the light changes. No familiar behavior works," he noted. "The sailor must weather these changes while anticipating the unknown."[184]

The Seamen's Church Institute has weathered the sea changes of the last 150 years. Now, like a well-found vessel, it confidently faces the unknown challenges of the 21st century.

Water Street Galleries: SCI's Art Collection

In 1993, the Institute opened its new Water Street Galleries with "All Ships Great and Small," an exhibit of model passenger and cargo ships culled from the Institute's distinguished maritime art collection of ship models. Many of the models had been in storage for more than twelve years, and this inaugural exhibit celebrated their coming home.

In 1916, after SCI's first large permanent headquarters building was built at 25 South Street, the Institute's supporters began decorating it with nautical artifacts that reflected the lives of seafarers. Over the years, the collections of ship models, marine paintings, nautical instruments, seafarer memorabilia, and other marine artifacts grew. Captain Ralph Cropley, who served on the board from 1908 to 1945, put together an eclectic group of international ship models donated by heads of state. Other models came from private collections. Still others were crafted by seafarers or brought home to SCI by them as souvenirs from ports around the world. Among this extensive collection are both merchant and naval vessels that represent commerce and sailing from the 16th century to the present. Several were created to scale by master model builders more than 200 years ago, before the days of naval architectural drawings.

By 1985, the Institute came to possess enough valuable marine art that the board moved to create, from its varied collections, a more focused group of objects. The remaining one-third of its acquisitions were auc-

The model of RMS Queen Mary arrives at SCI under the watchful eye of the Reverend Peter Larom (far right). The model was loaned by the South Street Seaport Museum for the "Rites of Passage" exhibition at SCI in 1993.

tioned at Christie's under the supervision of the attorney general. What remained went into storage during the Institute's sojourn in temporary headquarters at 50 Broadway.

Now the new Water Street building provides a splendid setting for the display of these maritime objects. Among the treasures that grace its corridors and enhance the nautical motif of the Institute's award-winning architectural design are oil paintings by Frank Vining Smith, Antonio Jacobsen, and other marine artists; prints of steamships by Currier and Ives and sloops by Fred S. Cozzens; and a collection of 18th-century European, hand-colored, marine engravings depicting important harbors and famous naval battles. Some of the more unusual items in the collection are examples of seafarers' art — macramé, knotted-rope picture frames, ships-in-bottles, embroidered ship portraits stitched with colored yarn, and watercolor sketches of tattoo designs. These offer a special insight into the complex, colorful, often lonely life of the professional seafarer.

A seafarer admires the builder's model for the *Vlissingen*, an 18th century Dutch frigate. The ship was built in 1754 at Vlissingen, the Netherlands.

SEAMEN'S CHURCH INSTITUTE

For those who are fascinated by the sea and sea lore, the Seamen's Church Institute's distinguished marine art collection of ship models, paintings, artifacts, and seafarers' memorabilia chronicles seafaring life. The Institute's Water Street Galleries provide display space for special pieces in the collection and other exhibits.

Nautical instruments from the days of early merchant sail also have a place in the collection. The ebony, brass, and ivory English octant, pictured here, is a forerunner of the modern sextant and dates to the early 19th century.

SEA CHANGES

This oil on canvas is of the *Thomas W. Lawson,* a collier ship. The artist is unknown.

Oil paintings of ships, such as this one by Antonio Jacobsen, add to the richness of the history of the seafarer. Jacobsen came to America from Denmark during the last quarter of the 19th century and painted through the first quarter of the 20th century.

These watercolor sketches of tattoo designs are among the most interesting objects in the Institute's collection.

Bibliography

"Addition to Seamen's Center Stresses Flexibility." *New York Times*, September 15, 1963.

"Admiral Mahan, Naval Critic, Dies." *New York Times*, December 2, 1914.

Ahlstrom, Sydney E. *A Religious History of the American People*. New Haven: Yale University Press, 1973.

Albion, Robert Greenhalgh. *The Rise of New York Port 1815-1860*. New York: Charles Scribner's Sons, 1939.

Albion, Robert Greenhalgh, and Jennie Barnes Pope. *Sea Lanes in Wartime: The American Experience 1775-1942*. New York: W.W. Norton & Company, Inc., 1942.

Ames, Lynne. "Grace Church Prepares to Say Farewell to a Local Legend." *New York Times*, June 28, 1992.

Balkin, Richard, ed. *The Everyday Life in America Series. Victorian America: Transformations in Everyday Life 1876-1915*, by Thomas J. Schlereth. New York: HarperCollins Publishers, 1991.

Balkin, Richard, ed. *The Everyday Life in America Series*. Vol. 2, *The Uncertainty of Everyday Life 1915-1945*, by Harvey Green. New York: HarperCollins Publishers, 1992.

Barber, Red. "Parachute Parson." *Episcopal Church News*, January 10, 1954.

Beckley, Zoe. "'Little Sister' of Sailors, Inventor of Boozeless Bar, Teaches Tars Fox Trot: Irene Katharine Lane, Who Works at the Seamen's Church Institute, Dispels a Few Well-Worn Superstitions About Mariners." *Saturday Evening Mail*, April 1915.

Boyer, Richard O. "Profiles: Joseph Curran." *The New Yorker*, July 6, 13, and 20, 1946.

Brouwer, Norman J. "The Port of New York, 1860-1985: Improving Conditions for Sailors, Ashore and Afloat." *Seaport*, XXIII, no. 2 (Fall 1989).

Brouwer, Norman J. "'Sailors Can Only Be Made Aboard Sailing Ships': Stephen B. Luce and the Federal Act of 1874." *Sea History*, 57 (Spring 1991).

Buckley, Christopher. *Steaming to Bamboola*. New York: St. Martin's Press, 1982.

Bunker, John. "From Holystones to Gantry Cranes: A Brief History of the Seamen's Church Institute of New York and New Jersey." 1978(?) TMs [photocopy]. The Seamen's Church Institute of New York and New Jersey.

Candee, Marjorie Dent. "Raymond Hall." Archives, The Seamen's Church Institute of New York and New Jersey.

Carroll, Raymond G. "Seamen's Institute in New York Example of How Multimillionaires Vie in Charity Work: J.P. Morgan gave 25,000 Toward Erection of 1,250,000 Building; Came Back With 50,000 More When J.D. Rockefeller Gave 50,000 — Proves Real Home for Sailors." *New York Evening Mail*, November 2, 1923.

Chapman, Paul K. *Trouble on Board: The Plight of International Seafarers*. Ithaca: ILR Press, 1992.

"Child Refugee Here is Hoping Against Raids: 118 in from Britain Put in a Day of Play While Homes Are Being Sought for Them." *New York Herald Tribune*, October 1, 1940.

"Clarence G. Michalis, Banker, Dead." *New York Times*, December 14, 1970.

Clark, William H. *Ships and Sailors: The Story of Our Merchant Marine*. Boston: L.C. Page & Co., 1938.

Crafton, Barbara. "Seamen's Church Institute is Sailors' Home Away From Home." *The Episcopalian*, April 1989.

Cranwell, John Philips. *Spoilers of the Sea: Wartime Raiders in the Age of Steam*. New York: W.W. Norton & Company, Inc., 1941.

Croy, Homer. "Old Doctor KDKF: A Remarkable Form of Long Range Medical Service that Uncle Sam is Developing to Cure the Sick and Injured on Ships Beyond the Reach of Surgeons." *Popular Radio*, October 1922.

Currier, Richard D. *The Sailor's Log*. New York: Legal Aid Society, 1906.

Dana, Richard Henry, Jr. *Two Years Before the Mast*. New York: Penguin Classics, 1986.

Dunlap, David. "Seamen's Institute Finds a Haven on Water Street." *New York Times*, October 31, 1988.

Dupin, Chris. "Seamen's Church Institute Improves Sailor's Lot." *Journal of Commerce*, March 4, 1985.

"Elizabeth Channel Completed." *New York Times*, October 24, 1961.

English, Merle. "'Abandoned' Ship Stuck With No Place for Cargo." *New York Newsday*, February 12, 1986.

Farnam, Henry W. "The Seamen's Act of 1915." *American Labor Legislation Review*, VI (1916).

"50 Cops Club Seaman at Institute." *New York Daily News*, August 19, 1932.

"50 Police Guard Benefit to Aid Seamen's Church." *New York Herald Tribune*, November 3, 1932.

"Fifty Years Marked by Port Newark." *New York Times*, October 21, 1965.

Finn, Jonathan. "Janet Roper: Mother to 50,000 Seamen." [1943] TMs [photocopy]. The Seamen's Church Institute of New York and New Jersey.

"Five More Ship Berths Planned in Jersey At Marine Terminal." *New York Times*, November 15, 1965.

"Foil Plot to Bomb Shipping in Harbor: Police Seize Five and Enough Explosives to 'Blow Up Half the Town' — One Confesses." *New York Times*, November 17, 1931.

"4 Are Injured In Free-for-All At Sea Institute: 3 Guards at Door Felled as Sailors Inside Join Attack by 12 in Street." *New York Herald Tribune*, August 19, 1932

Fraenkel, Shirley. "A Taste of the Real Thing: Seamen's Church Institute Trains Seamen on Simulator to Enhance their Effectiveness in Doing their Jobs." *VIA International*, April 1992.

"Free Haircuts for Sailors." *New York Sun*, November 8, 1932.

Furuseth, Andrew. "The Seamen's Law and its Critics." *American Labor Legislation Review*, VI (1916).

"Future of the Merchant Marine Sized Up By Chairman [Albert D.] Lasker [of U.S. Shipping Board]: Believes Private Operation Better than Governmental but Ships Must Run One Way or the Other — Where We Stand in Our Fight for International Trade." *New York Times*, May 20, 1923.

Goodbody, John C. *One Peppercorne: A Popular History of the Parish of Trinity Church*. New York: Trinity Church in the City of New York, 1982.

Hanlon, John. "Another Scope." *Providence Evening Bulletin*, June 28, 1970.

Harrington, John Walker. "Joint Committee Seeks $100,000 To Aid Seamen: Fund to Be Used to Care for 1,000 Now Believed Destitute in New York." *New York Herald Tribune*, November 8, 1931.

Healey, James C. "The Life of Archibald Romaine Mansfield, Apostle to Seamen." [1940] TMs [photocopy]. The Seamen's Church Institute of New York and New Jersey.

Healey, James C. "Sailors' Home and Institute." *Sailor's Magazine and Sailor's Friend*, May 1929.

Honig, Milton. "Hughes Dedicates First Section of Huge Elizabeth Project." *New York Times*, August 16, 1962.

Hugill, Stan. *Sailortown*. New York: E.P. Dutton & Co., Inc., 1967.

Huxtable, Ada Louise. "Downtown New York Begins to Undergo Radical Transformation." *New York Times*, 1967. Scrapbook. The Seamen's Church Institute of New York and New Jersey.

"Jack Ashore." *Harper's New Monthly Magazine*, no. CCLXXVIII, (July 1873).

James, Henry J. *German Subs in Yankee Waters: First World War*. New York: Gotham House, Inc., 1940.

"Juliana Greets Dutch Sailors: Visits Them at Seamen's Church Institute." *New York Sun*, December 21, 1940.

Jones, Charles J. *From the Forecastle to the Pulpit: Fifty Years Among Sailors*. New York: N. Tibbals & Sons,

Klein, Norman. "Idle Tars Have Depression Tied Up In Sailor's Knot." *New York Evening Post*, June 8, 1933.

Kverndal, Roald. *Seamen's Missions: Their Origin and Early Growth*. Pasadena: William Carey Library, 1986.

Lammers, Ann Conrad. "A Woman on the Docks." *Journal of Pastoral Care*, XXXVI, no. 4 (December 1982).

Lloyd, Barbara. "Matching Navigational Skills With a Computer." *New York Times*, November 28, 1988.

The Lookout. New York: The Seamen's Church Institute of New York and New Jersey, 1910 – present.

Lubbock, Basil. *The China Clippers*. Glasgow: James Brown & Son, Publishers, 1919.

Machalaba, Daniel. "Nautical Upheaval: Shipping Firms Suffer As Boat Values Decline and Freight Rates Fall." *Wall Street Journal*, November 5, 1985.

Maguire, John Arthur. *Lance of Justice: History of the Legal Aid Society, 1876-1926*. Cambridge: Harvard University Press, 1928.

Manchester, Herbert. *A Century of Service: The Seamen's Bank for Savings 1829-1929*. New York: The Seamen's Bank for Savings, 1929.

Manchester, William. *The Last Lion: Winston Spencer Churchill: Alone, 1932-1940*. Boston: Little, Brown and Company, 1988.

Mansfield, Archibald R. "Free Medical Aid by Radio Saves Lives On Vessels Far Out to Sea." *RCA NEWS*, August 1931.

A Maritime History of New York, compiled by workers of the Federal Writers' Project of the Work Progress Administration for the City of New York. New York: Haskell House Publishers, 1973.

Maske, Monica. "A Spiritual Port of Call for Seamen." *Newark Star Ledger*, November 9, 1979, reprinted in SCI's 146th *Annual Report*.

Massie, Robert K. *Dreadnought: Britain, Germany and the Coming of the Great War*. New York: Random House, 1991.

McKay, Richard C. *South Street: A Maritime History of New York*. New York: Haskell House Publishers, 1971.

Melville, Herman. *Redburn*. New York: Penguin Classics, 1986.

Monsarrat, Nicholas. *The Cruel Sea*. London: Penguin Books, 1951.

Moorehouse, Clifford P. *Trinity: Mother of Churches*. New York: The Seabury Press, 1973.

Morley, Raymond. "Our Merchant Marine." *Newsweek*, April 5, 1954. Reprinted in *The Lookout*, May 1954.

Morris, Jack H. "Though Styles Change, Cornerstones Endure — In One Form or Another." *Wall Street Journal*, August 5, 1968.

Morris, James. *The Great Port*. New York: Harcourt Brace & World, Inc., 1969.

Morris, Jan. *Manhattan '45*. New York: Oxford University Press, 1987.

Moscow, Alvin. *Collision Course: the* Andrea Doria *and the* Stockholm. New York: Putnam Publishing Group, 1959.

Mulligan, John M. "The Seamen's Church Institute Explains Its Facilities Move." *Villager*, July 4, 1968.

National Maritime Union of America, AFL-CIO. *The Story of the National Maritime Union of America, AFL-CIO*. Washington: Merkle Press, Inc., 1967.

Nevins, Allan, ed. *Diary of Philip Hone 1828-1851*. New York: Dodd, Mead and Company, 1927, (2 vols.).

Nevins, Allan, and Milton Halsey Thomas, ed. *Diary of George Templeton Strong*. New York: Macmillan, 1952.

"N.Y. Harbor Gets a New Landmark." *New York Times*, September 1, 1968.

"New York Nautical College Has Been Taken Over By the Seamen's Church Institute and Y.M.C.A." *New York Herald*, March 29, 1914.

"New Shipping Law Tested: Crew of the *John R. Kelly* Gets the Biggest Wages on Record." *New York Times*, March 14, 1899.

Nock, Albert, and Catherine Wilson. "Autobiography of the Rev. Dr. Archibald Romaine Mansfield." 1938 TMs [photocopy]. The Seamen's Church Institute of New York and New Jersey.

Norman, Michael. "Our Towns: A Frustrated Seaman in Clerical Garb." *New York Times*, June 9, 1985.

"NY Radar Training Conference To Be First Held in US." *Journal of Commerce*, August 30, 1985.

Oliver, Edward. "The Sea Rescue of the Century." *Ships and the Sea*, Winter 1957.

"On the Sun Deck: New Holland Room at Institute." *New York Sun*, November 18, 1940.

"On the Sun Deck: Refugee Children Take the Waterfront." *New York Sun*, October 2, 1940.

"118 British Child Refugees Here With Chins Up: They Proudly Tell of Raids That Missed, Minimizing Air Damage to London." *New York Herald Tribune*, September 30, 1940.

"Our Ships: An Analysis of the United States Merchant Marine" by the editors of *Fortune*. New York: Oxford University Press, 1938.

Parker, Benjamin C.C. Journal. AMs, 1843. The Seamen's Church Institute of New York and New Jersey.

Peterson, Maggie Walsh. "Farewell to the Seamen's Church Institute 1923-1968" [*sic!*]. *Villager*, June 13, 1968.

"Plunkett Pleads for Larger Marine: Admiral, in Two Navy Day Speeches, Stresses Need for Merchant Ships." *New York Times*, October 28, 1927.

"Police Thwart Reds at Theatre Benefit: 43rd Street Heavily Patrolled as Patronesses of Seamen's Church Institute Attend Play." *New York Times*, November 3, 1932.

"Port Authority Reports Progress in Marine Terminal Program." *New York Times*, July 16, 1961.

"Ports of Missing Men." *New York Times*, August 21, 1935.

Protestant Episcopal Church Missionary Society for Seamen (PECMSS) [Seamen's Church Institute of New York and New Jersey]. *Annual Report*, 1844.

PECMSS. "Minutes of the Superintending Committee of the Floating Church of Our Saviour 1843-1874." AMs. The Seamen's Church Institute of New York and New Jersey.

PECMSS. "Journal of the Floating Church." AMs, 1843. The Seamen's Church Institute of New York and New Jersey.

Rainsford, W. S., Alfred T. Mahan, and J. Augustus Johnson. "For Justice and Protection to Sailors: Report of Addresses Delivered at a Meeting Held at Sherry's." New York: PECMSS, 1902.

"Reds Raid Seamen's Home." *New York Mirror*, August 19, 1932.

Reinitz, Bertram. "Sailors Change Cellars of City: Wanderers of Deep Seas Find Care of Big Apartment Houses to Their Liking and Become Efficient Guardians." *New York Times*, January 20, 1929.

"Rev. R. S. Hall, 61, Paratroop Cleric." *New York Times*, June 24, 1970.

"The Sailor on Shore." *New York Post*, May 23, 1930.

"Sailors Shoes Yield Money to Bank: Hotel Guards Hard-Won Savings for Wanderers All Over the World." *New York World*, March 30, 1930.

"Sails Under a New Law: The *Emily F. Whitney* Gets a Crew After Fighting the 'Crimps.'" *New York Times*, March 7, 1899.

Schlesinger, Arthur M., Jr. *The Crisis of the Old Order 1919-1933: The Age of Roosevelt*. Boston: Houghton Mifflin Co., 1957.

Schofield, William G. *Eastward the Convoys*. Chicago: Rand McNally & Company, 1965.

"Seamen's Church Hotel Expands: Fourteen Branches [of the Seamen's Church Institute of America] Guide the Sailor and Help To See Justice is Done Him." *New York Sun*, February 7, 1928.

The Seamen's Church Institute of New York and New Jersey. *Annual Report*, 1844 – present.

"Seamen's Church Institute Begins Move to New Quarters." *New York Times*, February 9, 1968.

"Seamen's Home Mother Saves 3,000 Lost in 'The Ports of Missing Men': Mrs. Janet L. Roper Uses Detective Methods in Tracing Ocean Wanderers." *New York World*, September 2, 1931.

"Seamen's Museum Is to Close Without Berth on the Horizon." *New York Times*, July 2, 1967.

Selwitz, Bob. "Chaplain Has Diverse Congregation." *Journal of Commerce*, April 2, 1986.

Shipler, Guy Emory, Jr. "Evacuees: British Children Take Over Seamen's Institute." *The Churchman*, October 15, 1940.

"Shipowners' War Grows: Members of Maritime Exchange Committee on Admissions Out." *New York Times*, May 13, 1899.

Smith, Matthew Hale, ed. *Wonders of a Great City*. Chicago: People's Publishing Co., 1887.

Statutes at Large of the United States of America. Revised Statute Chap. 389, Sec. 4507, 4576, 4545, 4165, 5347. Vol. XXIX, 1897.

Sullivan, Allanna. "A 700-Foot Tanker Just Doesn't Handle Quite Like a Honda." *Wall Street Journal*, April 14, 1989.

A Symposium on Andrew Furuseth. New Bedford, MA: Darwin Press, 1948.

"Transport Events: Mail for Seamen." *New York Times*, June 16, 1968.

"Treatment by Radio of Ill Sailors in Mid-Ocean Was First Suggested by Captain at Seamen's Church Institute." January, 1924. Scrapbook. The Seamen's Church Institute of New York and New Jersey.

Tuchman, Barbara W. *The Proud Tower: A Portrait of the World Before the War 1890-1914*. New York: Macmillan Company, 1966.

Tuchman, Barbara W. *The Zimmermann Telegram*. New York: Ballantine Books, 1958, 1966.

"25 Seamen Ousted After Riot at Home: Police Raid Invaders of Institute in South Street After Special Officers are Beaten." *New York Times*, August 19, 1932.

"25 Seamen Raid Their Institute: Battle Police After Demanding Free Food for All — Four Men Injured." *World Telegram*, August 19, 1932.

Uhl, Robert. "They Got It All, and They Ain't Too Holy." *Seaport*, XVIII, no. 2 (Fall 1984).

U.S. House of Representatives, 55th Congress, 2d Session. "Laws Relating to American Seamen." Report No. 1657, July 8, 1898.

U.S. House of Representatives, 56th Congress, 1st Session. "Boarding of Vessels." Report No. 301, February 12, 1900.

U.S. Senate, 54th Congress, 1st Session. Report No. 832, May 2, 1896.

U.S. Senate, 56th Congress, 1st Session. "Boarding of Vessels." Report No. 33, January 4, 1900.

Valle, James E. "United States Merchant Marine Casualties in World War II." *American Neptune*, vol. 53, no.1, Winter 1993.

Van der Vat, Dan. *The Atlantic Campaign: The Great Struggle at Sea 1939-1945*. London: Hodder & Stoughton, 1988.

"Where Sailors Seek Safe Harbor When Ashore." *New York Sun*, January 17, 1915.

Whittemore, James R. "The Seamen's Church Institute: 150 Years and Beyond." D.Min. diss., New York Theological Seminary, 1985.

Young Men's Auxiliary Education and Missionary Society (YMAEMS) [The Seamen's Church Institute of New York and New Jersey], "Constitution and By-Laws Minutes 1834-1843." The Seamen's Church Institute of New York and New Jersey.

Notes

[1] Protestant Episcopal Church Missionary Society for Seamen (PECMSS), *First Annual Report*, 1844.

[2] Young Men's Auxiliary Education and Missionary Society (YMAEMS), July 18, 1842.

[3] YMAEMS, March 20, 1843.

[4] YMAEMS, May 1, 1843.

[5] Ahlstrom, 427.

[6] Bennett Tyler, *The New England Revivals . . . from Narratives First published in the Connecticut Evangelical Magazine* (Boston 1846); quoted in Ahlstrom, 415.

[7] Ahlstrom, 491.

[8] *The Lookout*, July 1934.

[9] Dana, 7.

[10] Melville, 111.

[11] Massie, 385.

[12] Melville, 203-5. Novaya Zemlya is an island off the arctic coast of Russia.

[13] PECMSS, *Annual Report*, 1845.

[14] PECMSS, *Annual Report*, 1846.

[15] McKay, 196.

[16] Possibly R. Lewis, Liquors, at 241 South Street, corner of Pike's Slip. See Doggett's New York City Directory for 1852, *South Street*, 432-50.

[17] PECMSS, "Journal of the Floating Church," July 17, 1843.

[18] Smith, 406-7.

[19] Parker, Journal, quoted in Bunker, 29.

[20] Parker, Journal, October 21, 1843.

[21] Nock and Wilson, 34-36.

[22] Melville, 77.

[23] Kverndal, 411.

[24] Nock and Wilson, 140-41; Uhl, 12.

[25] Hugill, 84.

[26] "Jack Ashore."

[27] Hugill, 87.

[28] Parker, Journal, January 28, 1844; quoted in Nock and Wilson, 80-81.

[29] PECMSS, "Minutes of the Superintending Committee of the Floating Church of Our Saviour 1843-1874," October 20 and 23, 1843.

[30] *The Evergreen*, April 1845, quoted in Uhl, 12.

[31] *The Evergreen*, April 1845, quoted in *The Lookout*, October 1982.

[32] PECMSS, *Annual Report*, 1878, quoted in Bunker, 55.

[33] Isaac Maguire, Journal, quoted in Bunker, 52.

[34] Maguire, Journal, August 19, 1883, quoted in Bunker, 53.

[35] *New York Times*, June 21, 1897.

[36] Nock and Wilson, 362.

[37] Nock and Wilson, 342.

[38] Nock and Wilson, 7.

[39] Nock and Wilson, 192.

[40] Nock and Wilson, 305.

[41] Nock and Wilson, 305.

[42] Nock and Wilson, 305.

[43] Nock and Wilson, 325.

[44] Nock and Wilson, 310.

[45] U.S. Cal. 1897, Rev. St. § 4598, 4599, authorizing the apprehension, imprisonment, and return on board of deserting seamen in the merchant service held valid; Robertson v. Baldwin, 17 S.Ct. 326, 165, U.S. 275, 41 L.Ed. 715.

[46] Nock and Wilson, 310.

[47] Nock and Wilson, 295.

[48] John Arthur Maguire, 137.

[49] Uhl, 14.

[50] Nock and Wilson, 300-1.

[51] "Public Acts of the Fifty-Fifth Congress of the United States," Chap. 28, "An Act to amend the laws relating to American seamen, for the protection of such seamen, and to promote commerce," approved December 21, 1898. *The Statutes at Large of the United States of America*, vol. XXX, Government Printing Office, ?date, 755-64.

[52] *New York Times*, March 7, 1899.

[53] Nock and Wilson, 339.

[54] Captain A.S. Pendleton, according to Mansfield, who also states that the *Whitney*'s owner was Charles Brewer.

[55] Tuchman, *Proud Tower*, 153.

[56] Quoted in Tuchman, *Proud Tower*, 149.

[57] *New York Times*, March 7, 1899.

[58] *New York Times*, March 14, 1899.

[59] *New York Times*, March 14, 1899.

[60] *New York Times*, May 13, 1899.

[61] *New York Times*, May 13, 1899.

[62] Healey, "The Life of Archibald Romaine Mansfield . . ," 91.

[63] Healey, 91.

[64] Reprinted in *The Lookout*, January 1915.

[65] Healey, 96.

[66] Healey, 94.

[67] *The Lookout*, June 1913.

[68] Healey, 97.

[69] Healey, 97.

[70] *The Lookout*, August 1917.

[71] Tuchman, *Zimmermann Telegram*, 192.

[72] James, 28.

[73] James, 28.

[74] Albion and Pope, 251.

[75] Uhl, 11.

[76] *The Lookout*, January 1923.

[77] *The Lookout*, May 1923.

[78] *Saturday Evening Mail*, April 1915.

[79] *New York Post*, May 23, 1930.

[80] *New York Sun*, January 17, 1915.

[81] *New York Evening Mail*, November 2, 1923.

[82] *New York Sun*, January 17, 1915.

[83] *New York World*, March 30, 1930.

[84] *The Lookout*, February 1918.

[85] *The Lookout*, September 1917.
[86] *The Lookout*, February 1920.
[87] *New York Times*, August 21, 1935.
[88] *New York Sun*, February 7, 1928.
[89] *The Lookout*, October 1920.
[90] *The Lookout*, April 1920.
[91] "Treatment by Radio of Ill Sailors in Mid-Ocean . . . ."
[92] Croy.
[93] *The Lookout*, June 1921.
[94] Croy.
[95] *New York Herald*, March 29, 1914.
[96] Scrapbook, January 1924, The Seamen's Church Institute of New York and New Jersey.
[97] *The Lookout*, July 1917.
[98] *The Lookout*, February 1921.
[99] *The Lookout*, January 1924.
[100] *The Lookout*, February 1922.
[101] *The Lookout*, May 1922.
[102] *New York Herald Tribune*, November 8, 1931.
[103] *New York Evening Post*, June 8, 1933.
[104] Schlesinger, 3.
[105] Bunker, 131.
[106] *New York Times*, November 17, 1931.
[107] Various newspaper reports, August 19, 1932.
[108] *New York Sun*, November 8, 1932.
[109] *New York Times*, February 13, 1934.
[110] Minutes of the board of managers, The Seamen's Church Institute, February 21, 1934.
[111] *The Lookout*, May, 1934.
[112] *The Lookout*, May, 1934.
[113] Finn, 183.
[114] Healey, "Sailors' Home and Institute."
[115] *New York World*, September 2, 1931.
[116] *The Lookout*, May 1943.
[117] *The Lookout*, October 1939.
[118] Manchester, 561.
[119] *The Lookout*, March 1942.
[120] *The Lookout*, March 1941.
[121] Schofield, 14-15.
[122] "'Ville de Liege' Survivors," *New York Sun*, December 2, 1941. Reprinted in *The Lookout*, January 1942.
[123] "Tankermen, 1942," *New York Times*, June 22, 1942. Reprinted in *The Lookout*, July 1942.
[124] *The Lookout*, May 1942.
[125] Van der Vat, 266.
[126] Van der Vat, 239.
[127] *The Lookout*, July 1944.
[128] Van der Vat, 382.
[129] Valle, 20.
[130] Van der Vat, 382.
[131] Valle, 20.
[132] *The Lookout*, October 1945.
[133] Raymond Morley, "Our Merchant Marine," *Newsweek*, April 5, 1954. Reprinted in *The Lookout*, May 1954.
[134] Minutes of the board of managers, The Seamen's Church Institute of New York and New Jersey, January 28, 1954.
[135] Jørgen U. Bjørge, "Report on Foreign-Flag Ship Visitation," January 9, 1956. The Seamen's Church Institute of New York and New Jersey.
[136] Jørgen Bjørge, Diary, November 21, 1957.
[137] Jørgen Bjørge, Diary, December 13, 1957.
[138] *New York Times*, December 14, 1970.
[139] Minutes of a meeting of the executive committee of the Seamen's Church Institute, February 14, 1958.
[140] *The Lookout*, June 1958; *Annual Report*, The Seamen's Church Institute of New York and New Jersey, 1958.
[141] *The Lookout*, August 1958.
[142] Minutes of a meeting of the board executive committee, July 30, 1958.
[143] *The Lookout*, December 1956.
[144] *The Lookout*, January 1957.
[145] Jørgen U. Bjørge, "Report on the Port Newark Station July 17, 1961, to July 24, 1961," July 31, 1961. The Seamen's Church Institute of New York and New Jersey.
[146] *The Lookout*, March 1955.
[147] *The Lookout*, December 1966.
[148] *Wall Street Journal*, August 5, 1968.
[149] *Villager*, June 13, 1968.
[150] *Villager*, July 4, 1968.
[151] *New York Times*, September 1, 1968.
[152] *New York Newsday*, February 12, 1986.
[153] *Wall Street Journal*, November 5, 1985.
[154] Monica Maske, "A Spiritual Port of Call for Seamen," *Newark Star Ledger*, November 9, 1979, reprinted in SCI's *146th Annual Report*, 1980.
[155] SCI, *146th Annual Report*, 1980.

[156] Conversation with Paul Chapman, May 20, 1993.
[157] *The Lookout*, June-July 1982.
[158] *The Lookout*, June-July 1982.
[159] *The Lookout*, June-July 1982.
[160] *The Lookout*, Summer 1993.
[161] *The Lookout*, Summer 1986; *The Episcopalian*, April 1989.
[162] *New York Times*, June 9, 1985.
[163] *Journal of Commerce*, April 2, 1986.
[164] *Journal of Commerce*, April 2, 1986.
[165] *The Lookout*, Fall 1992.
[166] *Annual Report*, The Seamen's Church Institute of New York and New Jersey, 1992.
[167] *New York Times*, June 28, 1992.
[168] *New York Times*, June 28, 1992.
[169] *New York Times*, June 28, 1992.
[170] *The Lookout*, Summer 1992.
[171] *Journal of Commerce*, March 4, 1985.
[172] *Journal of Commerce*, August 30, 1985.
[173] *The Lookout*, Fall-Winter 1985.
[174] *Wall Street Journal*, April 14, 1989.
[175] *Wall Street Journal*, April 14, 1989.
[176] *New York Times*, November 28, 1988.
[177] Fraenkel, *VIA International*, April 1992.
[178] *The Lookout*, Spring-Summer 1990.
[179] Whittemore, 6.
[180] SCI, *146th Annual Report*, 1980.
[181] *Annual Report*, The Seamen's Church Institute of New York and New Jersey, 1898.
[182] *The Lookout*, Spring 1985.
[183] *New York Times*, October 31, 1988.
[184] *Annual Report*, The Seamen's Church Institute of New York and New Jersey, 1991.

Photographic Credits

Andrea Laine—124

Anita and Steve Shevett—110, 112, 116

Dan Nerney—126, 127, 135

Fine Arts Collection, The Seamen's Bank for Savings—11

Flying Camera, Inc.—102

H.A. Schoonhals—120

Harpers XXVIII, No 1417—20

Jeff Goldberg/Esto—98, 100, 123, back cover

Katherine Andriotis—103, 104, 105, 106, 107, 121 (left)

Maritime New York in 19th Century Photographs—22

Museum of the City of New York—13

New-York Historical Society—2, 8, cover

The New York Public Library—9 (bottom)

Rochelle Ohrstrom—115

LEAH ROBINSON ROUSMANIERE is a freelance writer who lives in New York City and Stamford, Connecticut. She holds a degree in religion and philosophy, and for twelve years was associate registrar at Union Theological Seminary in New York City. Married to nautical writer John Rousmaniere, she has sailed along the New England coast, in the Caribbean, and in Alaska. She is the author of a medical thriller, *Blood Run*, published under the name Leah Ruth Robinson, and is at work on another. Leah's mother-in-law, Jessie Rousmaniere, for many years has been a knitter for SCI's Christmas-at-Sea program.